Empowering Everyone's Storms Of Inflation In Life: Make In Shrinkation

Empowering Everyone's Storms Of Inflation In Life: Make In Shrinkation

Glenn Colson

Copyright © 2024 by Glenn Colson.

Library of Congress Control Number: 2024918165
ISBN: Hardcover   979-8-3694-2909-9
           Softcover   979-8-3694-2910-5
           eBook   979-8-3694-2911-2

All rights reserved. No part of this book may be reproduced or transmitted in any form or by any means, electronic or mechanical, including photocopying, recording, or by any information storage and retrieval system, without permission in writing from the copyright owner.

Print information available on the last page.

Rev. date: 09/13/2024

To order additional copies of this book, contact:
Xlibris
844-714-8691
www.Xlibris.com
Orders@Xlibris.com
861469

Is It Possible to Face Inflationary Pressures?

About the Author

As an introduction, Glenn Colson is my name, and I am inspired to write this book to share with those who encounter financial challenges in life. A focus to maintain stability for independent financial objectives through means of choices to either working with elite companies or establishing ownership of business through ventures. I had a terrific mother, Annie M. Colson, who was married and raised nine children by herself. My siblings were Annette, Yvonne, Donna, Donald, Dennis, Morris, Norris, and Beatrice. Currently, Yvonne, Donna, Dennis, Norris, and Beatrice are living.

Despite my upbringing as a black man who lived in Newark, New Jersey, in the projects which was on Howard Street—a fight in the ghetto to resist be part of a drug dealer, participate in criminal activities participating carjacking, breaking in apartments, smoking marijuana, alcohol abuse, drug addiction, and etc.—not once did I ever in life drink liquor, indulge in using drugs, and involve myself in any illegal activities. As a church boy who most of my time I spent with my grandmother Ollie Leach, who brought me up in Miracle Temple Church, distracted my attention. She instilled productive positive energy spent time with me since I was the second oldest male.

At the age of seventeen, I attended Rutgers State University and got a bachelor of science degree in criminal justice and a master's in public health from Jones University.

All this I contribute to God and both my grandmother and mother. Struggling as a youngster, many obstacles I faced one particular challenge was depression. I was able to master the demon of depression through various methods. Various times as I was depressed, truly my outlets to defeat the battles using techniques were:

- Target Negativity and Eliminate
- Apply Listening
- Fight Only Essential Battles Not All
- Evaluate People's Backgrounds Learn from Their Errors
- Finding Humor and Laughter
- Breathing Exercises
- Stay Away from Angry Situations
- Visiting Church Services
- Work Overtime
- Planet Fitness Work Out

Just to give you a scenario of my upbringing living in the projects, I fought resisting the means of gang violence, drugs, etc. In addition, there was a riot; view the link:

https://youtu.be/2n0e3_vD-xE?si=EUgGDEcNw14xyFQo
America – Newark Riots (1967)

Note: This riot started on July 12, 1967, when I was six years old.

By the way, since I left Newark, New Jersey, FY-1993 was forced due to the City of New York required residency in order to continue employment, I have no regrets. Here is a sneak preview after leaving and pardon the profanity.

https://youtu.be/YRK021Mlzbg?si=wkLLXhYLDlMYQwyp
These Are the 10 Worst Neighborhoods to Live in Newark, New Jersey
https://youtu.be/kSv5z6EbmPg?si=RiXA9zmPFCfgWdTq
Newark New Jersey Most Violent Hood / Street Interview

I was blessed by God to obtain two properties Newark, New Jersey, at an early age of twenty-three; one property in South Orange, New Jersey; and at thirty-four years, a property in Woodside, New York.

One Family
52 West End Avenue
Newark, NJ 07106

Purchased	Recorded Date
05.04.1984	05.17.1984

Two Families
56 Hazelwood Avenue
Newark, NJ 07106

Purchased	Recorded Date
05.15.1984	06.11.1984

Two Families
1164 South Avenue
South Orange, NJ 07079
Purchased   **Record Date**
05.30.1985   06.10.1985

Two Families
48-41 58th Place
Woodside, NY 11377
Purchased   **Record Date**
06.25.2001   07.18.2001

During my journey through life, I learned to let go negativity and forgive people who constantly bring me down. Sharing my success with others should open ideas and utilize tools to overcome poverty. Building a financial structure will allow one to be independent and be stable in the purchase of property without worrying about a mortgage. Allowing success to spill over to assist others that need a boost in their career.

Dedication

I learned throughout the years to dedicate myself to happiness. Even though it is a struggle, one can be successful. People have behavior we cannot change; however, when you forgive, it assists your whole mindset of being a better person. That does not mean to be abused. Letting go by not holding grudges or gripes over people's behavior allows life to be able to control pressure. Of course, we do not forget our interactions with our enemies. However, part of the way to excel is to continue to move in an upward direction. Using techniques of being humble allows one to maintain happiness. Meekness is a key I discovered to a level of dignity. Dedication, which I practice, is giving back, assisting others, and not looking for rewards in exchange. Allowing giving back is a mirror image of yourself being sincere. Committing myself to be a guide for others to avoid critical problems in life.

Every balance of the ball is exclusive when fighting for matters in life. Instill within yourself the drive to become extraordinary ambassadors of success. For instance, where you reside, 98 percent of your time is required to be spent searching. In most cases, we encounter a time to satisfy our desire to settle in.

Some regrets stem from hurrying along, and cohesion took over; now we are stuck. These principles are like scales or adjusting weights on a piece of equipment when we work out. Easy weight sometimes produces no results. A little resistance shows no results, and striving with determination shows complete balance.

Results are noticeable, as we see many athletes, wrestlers, or muscle-bound individuals flex their muscles and demonstrate that hard work pays off. For instance, viewing past and current characters, such as:

Lana Kinnear

Lisa Moretti

Lorilyn Palmer

Simone Sherie

Adriana Gambino

Alexa Bliss

Crystal Waters

Undertaker

Austin Idol

Bo Dallas

Dwayne Johnson

Eddie Guerrero

Jerry Lawler

John Cena

Hulk Hogan

Randy Orton

Cody Rhodes

Roddy Piper

Dawn Staley

Maya Moore

Sue Bird

Becky Hammon

Breanna Stewart

Answer these questions truthfully:

Describe in your mind the weather conditions in the State of Alaska.

Now, if you lived in Florida during those six months and summers stayed in Arizona, would you appreciate the climate?

Going through depression and mishaps makes you appreciate moments of joy. Climbing up a mountain and observing the view is spectacular. Getting along and sharing neutral respect go a long way. Rough experiences prepared me for the future. Truly, I can attest that New York City is my mentor through challenges to rewarding and pulling resources from the opportunity. When I reach a certain level of success and the plateau is enormous, I would rather voluntarily and generously distribute my wealth with no strings attached. When I am deceased, there is no way to enjoy spending money once my eyes are shut tight.

I also implied five *P*s revolving around productivity, a breakdown as follows:

P — Proper

P — Preparation

P — Proactivity/Presence

P — Promotion

P — Prosperity

Acknowledgment

In honor of my oldest sister, **Annette Hicks,** who has two living sons, Jason Hicks and Craig Hicks, both of whom have children, and I admired her even though she was nine years older.

Famous things they implied were:

Keep your thoughts positive because your thoughts become your words. Keep your words positive because your words become your behavior. Keep your behavior positive.

Find people's time and give them space. Don't beg anyone to stay. Let them roam; what is meant for you will always be yours.

In honor of both my brothers, **Morris Colson** and **Donald Colson**.

Don't carry your mistakes around with you. Instead, place them under your feet and use them as stepping stones to rise above them. Your mind will always believe everything you feel.

Feed it faith.

Feed it truth.

Feed it with love.

Donna Colson is my sister as well as a mother of two children. Proudly, her daughter has a master's, and her son has a bachelor of science, and Donna is the grandmother of three grandchildren. Her saying in life is "not performing to my expectations" and dreams don't work unless you do the work. Other aspirations she implied don't ruin a new day by dwelling on yesterday and a few others listed below:

Let It Go

A clear rejection is always better than a false promise.

The more chances you give someone, the less respect you get; they will begin to ignore the standards that you've set because they will know another chance will always be given. They're not afraid to lose you because they know they will be forgiven no matter what you want. Walk away when they get comfortable with depending on your forgiveness.

Dennis Colson, my brother, and Leslie Colson, the mother of his daughter and son. I admire him; this man owes no money on his property; he's very clever and can take a car apart and put it back together. Leslie, I give her credit as the wife and husband. Both have given me inspirations. For instance, stress: It's not what happens to us. It's our response to what happens, and response is something we can choose. Empty minds make the most noise.

Three things cannot be long-hidden: the sun, the moon, and the truth.

There is something that is greater than the world. It will begin to *energize*. Sustain your existence if you leave it now; that is why I believe that you are great, that there's something magnificent about you. Regardless of what has happened to you in your life, regardless of how young or how old, you think properly, take life day by day, and be grateful for the little things. Don't get caught up in what you can't control focus on the positive.

Yesterday is not ours to recover; tomorrow is ours to win or lose. Never let a stumble in the road be the end of the journey!

Norris Colson, my brother who is a father of one daughter and one son. Unfortunately, the son who passed away is still remembered. As a result, he has ten grandchildren. To carry a mind of understanding, both encouraged me with attitudes to follow a philosophy. The way to get started is to quit talking and begin doing. Be yourself; everyone else is already taken. Always forgive your enemies; nothing annoys them so much. Most of the problems in life are because of two reasons: we act without thinking or we keep thinking without acting. You don't need someone to complete you; you only need someone to accept you completely.

Our most memorable positive moments are dominated by four elements:

1. Elevation
2. Insight
3. Pride
4. Connection

Beatrice Colson is my baby sister. Definitely, I listened to her viewpoints on life. When you hate someone, they're still in your mind, and that tension steals the happiness of your life. That person who you hate has your life's happiness in control of her and his hands.

Seven types of people you need to completely avoid:

1. Gossips
2. Jealous haters
3. Time-wasters

4. Money-grubbers
5. Oversensitive
6. Excuse-makers
7. Miseducated

There is only one thing in the world worse than being talked about, and that is not being talked about. Always be positive because your values become your destiny.

Become your habit; keep your habits and your values positive. Yvonne Colson, who is one of my favorite sisters who I admire, has ten children and a total of thirteen grandchildren. I follow through with her aspects on life to be subjective and not to be tied down with objective. Progressive support systems are essential and even though we have an enormous family. Truly, we may not all get along; however, I can assure you that we stick together as a team to defend from others that may cause us harm. Trust no one because God is the answer. Believe in hope, in faith, despite what comes your way. Stay calm in all situations. Prosperity shall be with you in time, which you will encounter. Drown yourself in peace and harmony. Love and keep faith, climb the ladder, and still stay humble in your spirit. Everyone needs attention and to be listened to.

In memory of my brother, Morris Colson, who had two children. I recalled him saying "We will be in touch, stay vibrant, live with integrity," "Class has not anything to do with imagination but actions," "Change your prospective in life, instead of saying 'I got to deal with work' or 'I got to cope with struggles,' say 'I get an opportunity to go to work' and 'I get the first chance to learn how to manifest to go around road blocks.'"

Cousins

Darlene Higgs encourages methods masters of dark negative trends we drown 95 percent conclusive of nature; however, exclusive success upstream revolves around eternal 200 percent of progression. Marlene Higgs, who never used profanity in anger. She would make me laugh by saying, "Take a long walk off a short bridge," or "I didn't invent the wheel, I just learned how to drive it differently," or when a person confronted her at times, she would say, "The only thing I want to see is the back of your head and heels." Darlene Higgs said, "We all done dirt, but it is something you steam road ahead and rise above." Jeanie Higgs, I am always reminded that her philosophy is "Life is a journey: 10 percent is happiness and 90 percent is how you respond." Aaron Higgs, great talker with inspiration to stay calm in the storm, promotes a way in life which is adjacent to breaking barriers.

Pamela Green is a good woman of stature, standing strong and firm as a dedicated Christian lady, who also impressed me with her diverse background and supporting role model in life for others. A tale way theme that always reflects and echoes in my mind: the inspiration and steadfast task. She instilled in me a phase which I carry: "Now faith is the substance, hope for the evidence of things not seen," located in the Bible Hebrews 11:1–6. Also, as I cease negative compacts, she reminded me of an essential passage, "I can do all things through Christ which strengthens me" found in Philippians 4:13.

My first love, Barbara Hutchins, has been an icon in my life. As a person who always worked hard and maintained success in her life, I truly respect her. Former wife Amma Love Colson is a great affiliation and support.

Obviously, I must credit the drive for several years a good associate and friend Iris Ford known as Pepa an inspirational person who I known over 21 years. Her truth and guidance and philosophy in life implanted tremendous thoughts in my mind to write this book. She expresses her dream is to see people excel and live life to its fullest.

Objective is people hurting one another definitely she despises this is a wicket and inhuman act against one another. Remarkably her dedication within the workforce 25 years in the workplace. Truly, the clients that she works with not only did she inspire them obviously they motivate her. Interacting with the public her method to be successful she shared with others is "the job that you are hired. Make certain it is a passion whereas you are delighted instead of worrying about making lots of money."

Contrary to disappointments: fear: ignorance: negative objectives: sadness: and unsuitable variations. As a matter-of-facts, these traits are vital as a winding worldview journey in our lives. She is intrigue with the privilege that it is an honor to demonstrate that within life you do have the insensitive to channel through challenges.

Using tons of resources by shredding obstacles and keeping the foot on the accelerator using the prospective green light to move ahead. Placing the foot on the brake as you approach the red light to end the impossibilities. This stamps out all mishaps by continuing to drive looking forward and not back.

Contents

About the Author vii
Dedication xi
Acknowledgment xxv

Chapter 1 Introduction...1
Chapter 2 Purpose in Life..5
Chapter 3 Financial Strategies..12
                Financial Strategies..14
Chapter 4 Exclusive Prohibited Gatekeeper 33
Chapter 5 Legal Protections 42
                Legal Routes 45
                Challenges and Considerations 46
Chapter 6 Recognition...48
                Families in a Rural Texas Town Adopted
                Seventy-Seven Children This Couple Led
                the Way..56
Chapter 7 Philosophies and Strategies.........................103
                Armless Girl Jessica Cox Gains Pilot's License... 114
Chapter 8 Employment Opportunities 115
                Exploring Career Paths 116
                Emerging Frontiers......................................118
                Beyond Traditional Jobs 118

	New York Safety Educator – Driving Instructor Sponsorship Program	119
Chapter 9	Conclusion	150
	Why You Need This Book (Especially Now) in the Face of Persistent Inflation	151

Index 153

Chapter 1

Introduction

It's hard to ignore the constant chatter about inflation in the news these days. The term is everywhere, from the headlines we read to the emails we receive, all talking about the rising prices that are impacting our daily lives. Inflation is a formidable foe, a mountain of ever-increasing prices that threatens to bury our financial dreams. It's important to understand the very nature of this beast we face. Inflation, as defined by Nobel Laureate in Economics Milton Friedman, is a sustained increase in the general price level of goods and services in an economy over time. This translates to a decrease in the purchasing power of a given unit of currency, which can impact both consumer budgets and business operations.

This book is your battle manual, packed with strategies to help you strengthen your grip on the rope. And it is not a one-size-fits-all solution. The financial realities of a New

Yorker differ greatly from those living in a rural Montana town. However, the core principle remains the same: we are all stronger together. This book equips you with the tools and strategies to navigate inflation, regardless of your location.

This is why when it comes to the universality of inflation, the first thing we must all remember is that you're not alone in this fight. Millions of people all around the world, in our states, cities, towns, and even our neighborhoods, are facing the same financial squeeze caused by inflation. We're all in this together, and we can use our shared experience as a way to boost our spirits.

Think of it like a global or, in our case, a national game of tug-of-war. On one side, we have rising costs that are pulling our financial security down. On our side, we have the power of calmness, resourcefulness, and a dash of "never give up" spirit.

Staying calm is essential because panic clouds judgment. When we're stressed, we tend to make impulsive decisions that can make things worse. Instead, let's channel the spirit of a kangaroo. Imagine this powerful marsupial, muscles coiled, ready to propel itself forward with a powerful leap. That's the energy we want to cultivate. We'll jump over inflation's hurdles, soaring high above the storm with a clear focus on the future.

This isn't about ignoring the challenge or pretending it doesn't exist. It's about acknowledging it, taking a deep breath, and saying, "Bring it on!" We'll confront this enemy pricing head-on, not with fear but with a strategic plan. We'll develop a financial war chest filled with actionable steps to minimize risk and weather the storm.

The current inflationary wave can be attributed to a confluence of factors, some unique to our times. The lingering effects of the global pandemic have disrupted supply chains, leading to shortages and price hikes on raw materials and finished goods. Additionally, expansionary monetary policies implemented during the pandemic, while necessary to stimulate economic recovery, have also contributed to increased money supply, fueling inflationary pressures.

It's important to remember that historical context is crucial. We can learn valuable lessons from past inflationary periods, such as the stagflationary environment of the 1970s, characterized by high inflation and stagnant economic growth. Economists like former Federal Reserve Chair Arthur Burns grappled with policy decisions that attempted to curb inflation while fostering economic growth, highlighting the delicate balancing act policymakers face.

To navigate this current inflationary period, just remember, "Never ever, never give up, keep calm and give back and be a blessing to others." I know this *staying calm* advice might seem like an unhelpful suggestion during difficult times, but it's actually a crucial first step. Panic and impulsive decisions can worsen the situation. The profession must adopt a multifaceted approach. One way to do this is to embrace data-driven decision-making. Analyzing the impact of inflation on your specific industry and target market can help you make informed decisions about your business operations. Another important step is to explore cost-saving measures without sacrificing quality or innovation. Lean manufacturing principles, popularized by Japanese management consultant Taiichi Ohno, can be instrumental in identifying and eliminating waste within production processes. Additionally, consider alternative suppliers or renegotiate existing contracts to mitigate the impact of rising costs.

It is important to keep a close eye on costs when running a business. However, focusing solely on cutting costs while ignoring potential revenue streams could prove to be a serious mistake. In order to ensure sustainable growth, it is essential to explore ways to adjust pricing models without alienating your customers. One way to achieve this is by employing revenue management techniques as described in academic journals such as Kotler, Keller, et al. (2022), Marketing Management. By analyzing market demand and competitor behavior, you can optimize your pricing strategies to maximize revenue.

It is also worth noting that inflation is often a broader trend that affects multiple businesses within the same industry. It is something that affects everyone. So within this calmness lies another crucial element: *giving back*. It may seem counterintuitive during challenging times, but extending a helping hand, even a small one, can be incredibly uplifting.

Maybe you offer to help a neighbor with their groceries or mentor a younger colleague struggling to budget. Acts of kindness, no matter how seemingly insignificant, create a ripple effect. They remind us that we're all in this together, and that by supporting one another, we build a stronger, more resilient community. To tackle this issue, consider forming strategic partnerships or collaborations with other businesses. This approach, known as coopetition, was first coined by business strategists Adam Brandenburger and Barry Nalebuff. By working together, you can negotiate bulk discounts with suppliers, streamline logistics, and ultimately create a mutually beneficial situation for all parties involved.

CHAPTER 2

Purpose in Life

Have you ever stared up at the night sky, a million tiny pinpricks of light against the vast darkness, and wondered, "Why am I here? What's my purpose in all this?" It's a question that has crossed all our minds at some point, especially during times of struggle. Right now, with inflation looming large, it's easy to feel lost and overwhelmed.

But here's the truth I believe in: we were all born to serve, not in a grand, sweeping way but in the everyday moments. Maybe it's helping a neighbor carry grocery, mentoring a younger colleague, or simply offering a listening ear to a friend facing their own financial woes. These acts of service, big or small, connect us and remind us that we're not alone.

This journey of conquering inflation isn't just about numbers on a spreadsheet; it's about our collective well-being. And that includes our mental health. Let me tell you a story.

My name is Glenn Colson, and like many of you, I've battled depression. During those dark times, the weight of the world felt crushing. Even the simplest tasks seemed insurmountable. It wasn't just the rising costs; it was the feeling of losing control, of watching my carefully planned budget crumble under the pressure of inflation. But I learned to fight back, not just for myself but for the purpose I discovered: helping others navigate their own storms.

Unfold a unique etiquette method that ceases criticizing people. As you observe children attempting to walk, they inevitably encounter encouragement step-by-step until they walk systematically, leap, and run. When you criticize me for this book, I am thrilled to know that your unproductive negativity boosts my challenges, and I thank you for the opportunity.

Enemies serve as a source of excelling; I keep them close by proxy within my circle. These clashes help in hammering out unsettled matters.

Empowering Everyone's Storms Of Inflation In Life: Make In Shrinkation

Look at Dr. Martin Luther King Jr.'s struggles in life; his legacy lives on. Nelson Mandela, who endured twenty-seven years in prison for opposing South Africa, is an icon. These men, like others, provide me with the strength not to look back and drown myself in folks who attempt tactics to make me fall.

We have choices in life: to be abused, allow the accuser or accusers to trample on us, or accept the role of a victim due to the potential of not being proactive.

Genuine respect is something enforced with people, including family members, irrespective of coworkers. Those whom I encountered disrespectful actions, such as bullying, discrimination, favoritism, harassment, hostility, hostile environments, and recently, age discrimination. Even as I stand alone in these ongoing battles, it appears in their eyesight I am looked upon as an outstanding sore thumb. When you stand up for what is correct, especially when federal laws are in place, some people disregard it. If you look back in history, Rosa Parks, best known as the Mother of the Civil Rights Movement, was a black woman who had the endurance and courage to refuse to give up her seat for a Caucasian. When the bus driver ordered her to stand up and threatened to have her arrested, she remained seated at the window and was not moved by his threat. I admired her; mainly, she had a quiet demeanor and responded, "You may do that."

As I reflect upon the truth, which most people would endlessly disagree with me, your negative actions interacting with others will entertain rewards of consequences or, best known worldwide, karma. For instance, here in New York City, some customers are comfortable boarding the buses and trains without paying. Eventually, the MTA collectively will end this free ride disposition when summonses are issued.

Many people, some who adopt an attitude of "I can ride free," carry it over into their lives and, if they happen to go to another state, will cope with repercussions. For instance, I am originally from New Jersey. If I joined a gang's carjacking and got caught in New Jersey, I would face a punishment of ten to thirty years of imprisonment, including at least five years without eligibility for parole. Let's say, lucky me, I never got caught, and if I did in New York State, the punishment would be that regardless of the situation, the offense is classified as a federal offense, and I would prepare to face as much as twenty-five years in prison.

Behavior with people never fails; let us take a look at carjacking in Michigan. People settle down and move on to Michigan, and their teenagers decide to impress friends by carjacking. According to the law, if found, the person is subject to a felony criminal conviction and a possible sentence of life imprisonment.

No one traveling by airline would enter the gate without paying. Various states will not tolerate it.

Here's the thing, inflation can trigger a similar feeling of helplessness. Sure, we all hear about the big mental health battles—depression, anxiety, the whole nine yards. But let's talk real. Right now, financial stress feels like a persistent low-grade fever zapping our energy and making even the smallest decisions feel monumental. Even adding anything to the shopping cart these days feels like a rebellious act. Every bleep of the scanner sounds like a tiny financial riot and the receipt? A manifesto of rising prices.

So in the spirit of service, let's explore some tools to combat negativity and depression, especially during challenging times.

- **Target Negativity:** Are those negative thoughts swirling in your head? Acknowledge them, then let them go. Focus on the positive steps you can take to improve your situation.
- **Active Listening:** Sometimes, the best way to help ourselves is to help others. Lend a listening ear to a friend or family member struggling with inflation.
- **Picking Your Battles:** Life throws a lot at us, but not every fight is worth our energy. Learn to discern between essential battles and those best left uncontested.
- **Learn and Move On:** Mistakes happen. Don't beat yourself up. Learn from them and move forward.
- **Find Humor:** Laughter is the best medicine, even during tough times. Watch a funny movie, read a comic strip, or share a joke with a friend.
- **Breathe:** Deep breathing exercises can calm your mind and body. Take a few minutes each day to simply focus on your breath.
- **Avoid Toxic Situations:** Distance yourself from negativity. Find supportive people who uplift you, not drag you down.
- **Spiritual Connection:** For some, faith offers solace and strength. Connect with your spiritual community if that brings you comfort.
- **Find Your Passion:** Hobbies and activities can provide a welcome escape and a sense of accomplishment.

Explore your interests, whether it's painting, gardening, or playing music.

- **Move Your Body:** Exercise is a powerful tool for boosting mood and overall well-being. Go for a walk, run, ride a bike, or hit the gym.

Remember, like I said in the first chapter, you're not alone in this battle. Financial struggles can exacerbate everyday challenges. But taking care of your mental well-being is just as important as managing your finances.

A healthy mind is a strategic mind, after all.

There are many resources available to help you maintain mental well-being during financial struggles. Here are a few places to start:

- **The National Alliance on Mental Illness (NAMI):** https://www.nami.org/Home offers free support groups and information on finding affordable mental health services.
- **The Substance Abuse and Mental Health Services Administration (SAMHSA):** https://www.samhsa.gov/ provides a national helpline (1-800-662-HELP) and resources for finding treatment.

I am not saying stop thinking about finances and bills and inflation that induce stress. But when you do think about it, think about keeping your mind at peace. By prioritizing both, you'll be better equipped to weather this storm and emerge stronger on the other side.

CHAPTER 3

Financial Strategies

The economic landscape these days feels like a monsoon on steroids—unpredictable, relentless, and capable of drenching even the most careful plans. Inflation, the ever-rising tide, threatens to wash away our purchasing power, while layoffs, like sudden flash floods, can leave us scrambling for financial stability.

For adults growing up in America of today, the America post-pandemic, these challenges hold a particular sting. We're a generation brimming with ambition, often juggling student loans, family responsibilities, and the dream of building a secure future. But inflation and layoffs can feel like a one-two punch, knocking the wind out of our carefully crafted financial plans.

However, here's the good news: we're not powerless. By prioritizing *financial planning*, we can build a robust *safety net* and we fight for what matters: security, dignity, and a future where bills don't induce panic attacks. Financial planning is a holistic and empowering process that can provide you with a sense of ease, control, and resilience. By adopting these strategies, you can confidently navigate the ups and downs of the economic world and continue pursuing your dreams, even when the winds of change may blow unexpectedly:

- **Anticipate the Enemy:** By understanding inflation trends and potential job market fluctuations, you can make informed decisions about your finances. This foresight is your early warning system, allowing you to adjust your spending habits and savings goals before the storm hits.
- **Fortify Your Defenses:** Building an emergency fund is your first line of defense. Having a buffer of 3–6 months' worth of living expenses can help you navigate unexpected job losses or medical emergencies without falling prey to high-interest debt.
- **Diversify Your Interests:** Putting all your financial eggs in one basket is a risky proposition. A diversified portfolio, with investments spread across different asset classes (stocks, bonds, real estate), can help mitigate losses if one area of the market takes a hit.
- **Sharpen Your Skills:** Investing in your professional development through additional training or certifications can make you a more valuable asset in the job market, increasing your employability and resilience during layoffs.

Financial planning isn't just about numbers and spreadsheets; it's about *empowerment and peace of mind*. It allows you to take control of your financial future, navigate challenges with confidence, and continue pursuing your dreams even when the economic winds shift.

Financial Strategies

Investment

Most people, when they receive a settlement, spend all their monies, which will not return. An investment to study an area with busy customers. Secure your business with cameras and video footage. Purchase a building and open a twenty-four-hour coinless laundry mat; this idea is credited to Pamela Green.

Employment Opportunities/Positions/Titles

- Airline Pilot
- Architecture
- American Red Cross
- Anesthesiologist
- Bank Teller
- Barber
- Building Manager
- Building Superintendent
- Bus Operator
- Cable Technician
- Car Mechanic
- Certified Nurse Assistant
- Chef
- Central Intelligence Agency
- Cleaner Worker
- Counselor
- Correction Officer
- Customer Service
- Cyber Security
- Daycare
- Deaf-Mute International Interpreter (Sign Language)
- Doctor (New York University Grossman Admissions; becoming a physician Tuition Free)

The Office of Admissions has been experiencing a high email influx regarding general admissions, including an extremely large number of emails from individuals inquiring about general application eligibility requirements. To ensure we provide the timeliest of responses to those individuals currently applying to NYU School of Medicine, we ask those individuals to resend your email with "Current Cycle" and your AMCAS ID in the subject line so that we may prioritize our reply to you.

For all other queries, please visit our website https://med.nyu.edu/education/md-degree/md-admissions, where you can learn more about how to apply, see our admissions requirements, and view our admissions timeline. For more information about Financial Aid at NYU School of Medicine, you may visit https://med.nyu.edu/education/md-degree/md-affordability-financial-aid. Please note all applications to our school must be submitted through AMCAS.

We wish you the very best in your pursuit of becoming a physician!

The Office of Admissions and Financial Aid

NYU School of Medicine

The Kaiser Permanente School of Medicine will temporarily cover all tuition and fees for its first five classes of students from 2020 to 2024. Unfortunately, the forty-eight to fifty students admitted annually must finance an estimated $34,500 in living expenses for the Pasadena, Calif., campus.

- Dog Walker
- Driver Instructor
- Driver Technician (Diversified Orthotics 3058 East Tremont Avenue Bronx, NY 10461 [718] 409-6280)
- Drug Counselor
- EKG Technician
- Elevator Repair Mechanic
- Emergency Medical Technician
- Engineer
- Federal Bureau Investigator Agent
- Fire Fighter
- Flight Attendant
- Foster Care
- Funeral Director

- Gardner
- Gas and Electric Technician
- General Contractor
- Greeter Representative
- Hairstylist
- Home Attendant
- Home Health Aide
- Insurance Agent
- Judge
- Journalist
- Landry Mat Worker
- Language Interpreter
- Lawyer (accident, corporate, criminal, housing, malpractice, or union representing workers that get no support from unions)
- Licensed Practice Nurse
- Life Coaching
- Life Guard
- Lyft and Uber Driver (car dealerships, medical facilities, etc.)
- Maintenance Worker Operator
- Military Services
- Movers
- Musical Singer and Writer
- National Notary Association
- Parking Lot Owner
- Pharmacy
- Phlebotomy Technician
- Physical Therapist
- Physician Assistants

- Private Investigator
- Probation Officer
- Process Server
- Professor
- Prosthetics Technician
- Psychiatrist Facilitator
- Real Estate Broker
- Real Estate Sales Associate/Salesperson
- Registered Nurse *Free Tuition

University of Rochester School of Nursing

The UR Nursing Scholars Program, launched in August, waives tuition for students enrolled in the school's accelerated bachelor's degree program.

- Restaurant Server
- Salvation Army
- Seamstress/Tailor
- Seasonal Worker
- School Teacher Instructor
- Scientist
- Security Officer
- Sheriff Officer
- Social Worker
- Storage Facility
- Technician Support
- Train Conductor
- Truck Driver
- Veterinary
- Weather Caster

- Wedding Planner
- Zoology

Building Business Relations

- American Cancer Society
- Churches
- Colleges and Universities
- Heart Foundation
- Veteran Administration

Preliminary Business Ventures

- Barber Shop

Sophisticated Investors

- Food Truck Operator Vendor (specialized dietary blood pressure and diabetes)
- Franchises Owners (Burger King, home health care facilities, McDonald's, Planet Fitness, etc.)
- Grocery Stores
- Land Mobile Home Community Owner
- National Notary
- Property Tax Liens
- Roller Skating Rank
- Storage Unit

Public Service References

- African Services Committee
- 429 W 127th Street

- New York, NY 1002
- 1 (212) 222-3882

To inquire if they sell African artwork.

Airlines Discounts

- Website: Skiplagged.com
- Trip.com
- Penny Savers
- Go three months before booking
- Ticket Window Hours Daily
  - (6:00 a.m.–9:00 a.m.)
  - (3:00 p.m.–6:00 p.m.)

Discount Penny Fairs

- Go in person before registering flight
- Air Pilots Cab in New York
- Joby Flies Quiet Electric Air Taxi in New York City
- www.jobyaviation.com

Electric Air Taxis Could Fly In New York City Skies As Soon As 2025

- New Jersey Transit Reduces Fare
- Half Fare Disable / Sixty-Two Years or Older
- https://www.njtransit
- (973) 491-7512
- (973) 275-5555

Glenn Colson

Public Service References

- New York City 311
- https://portal.311.nyc.gov
- (212) 639-9673
    - Borough Presidents
    - Community Boards
    - City Council Members
    - District Attorneys
    - Food Bank Resources
    - Free Taxes Preparation
    - House of Representatives
    - Housing Remedies
    - Members of the State Assembly and State
    - MTA Half Fare
    - Substantial Resources
    - Housing References

DRE—Disability Rent Income Exemption

Qualifications

- Must be eighteen years or older
- Disable
- Live in a rent-stabilized apartment
- Annual income $50,000.00

SCRIE—Senior Citizen Rent Increase Exemption

Qualifications

- Must be sixty-two years old or older

- Live in a rent-stabilized building
- Annual Income $50,000.00

SCHE — Senior Citizen Home Exemption

- Must be sixty-five years old
- Property owner
- Annual Income $58,399.00
- Eligibility tax reduction 5%–10%

*Owner exemption for tax

New York City Police Department

- Aviation Unit
- 50 Aviation Road
- Brooklyn, NY 11234
- (718) 692-1220
- United Youth Aviators: NYPD officers teach New York kids

Brooklyn Teens Graduate from the NYPD Aviation Program

- New York University Grossman School of Medicine
- Candidate Physicians No Tuition
- (212 263-5290

For all other queries, please visit our website, https://med.nyu.edu/education/md-degree/md-admissions, where you can learn more about how to apply, see our admissions requirements, and view our admissions timeline. For more information about Financial Aid at NYU School of Medicine, you may https://med.nyu.edu/education/md-degree/md-affordability-financial-aid. Please note all applications to our school must be submitted through AMCAS.

Small Business Services

- New York City Small Service Hotline
- (888 727-4692
- (212) 618-8810

New York Safety Educator

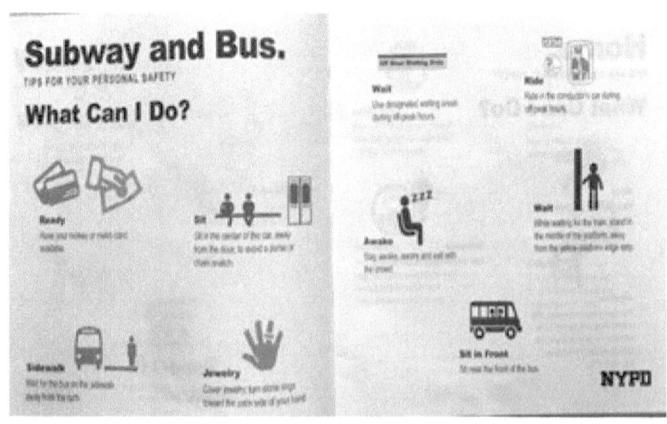

Empowering Everyone's Storms Of Inflation In Life: Make In Shrinkation

- Start your small business on Turo in New York
- Turo - Rent your car daily
- Vending Machines

Websites References

- Academy of Aviation
- https://www.academyofaviation.com

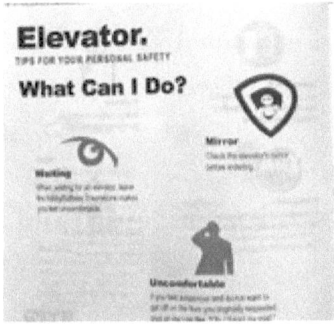

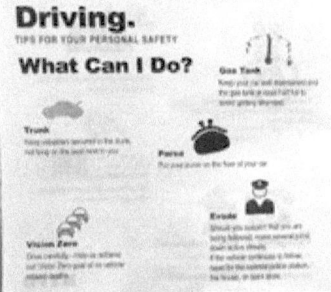

Glenn Colson

Aviation and Job Training Resources for Youths

Aviation Programs
NYPD Officers Teach Inner-City Kids to Fly Through Youth Aviation Programs

- Description: NYPD officers Milton Davis, and others, teach inner-city kids how to fly through youth aviation programs.

References

- ABC7 New York: NYPD officers teach inner-city kids to fly through youth aviation program (https://abc7ny.com/united-youth-aviation-program-nypd-kids-how-to-fly/12741059/)
- YouTube: Brooklyn Teens Graduate from NYPD Aviation Program (https://www.youtube.com/watch?v=PmsuOLBqwQc)

Commercial Pilot Programs—Adults and Kids Pilot Classes

- Website: Find Lost Money - New York State (https://www.ny.gov/services/find-lost-money-new-york-state)

Joby Aviation

- Website: www.jobyaviation.com (https://www.jobyaviation.com)

Empowering Everyone's Storms Of Inflation In Life: Make In Shrinkation

Invent Help

- Website: www.inventhelp.com (https://www.inventhelp.com)

Iris House

- Address: 2348 Adam Clayton Powell Junior Boulevard, New York, NY 10030
- Phone: (646) 548-0100
- Website: www.irihouse.org (https://www.irihouse.org)

Job Corps (Free Job Training Ages 16–24)

- Website: info.joinjobcorps.com (https://info.joinjobcorps.com)

The Flex Jobs Weekly Newsletter

Tomorrow is our Remote Work Virtual Job Fair, and we really hope you're planning to join us! It's an excellent way to get yourself directly in front of great employers who are hiring for either fully remote or hybrid positions right now.

Over the past few years, remote work has become the norm for so many, and employees want it to stay. While some businesses are initiating versions of RTO ("return to office"), lots of others are integrating remote and hybrid work arrangements into their company cultures and norms.

To highlight some of the leaders doing so, we recently released our annual list of the Top 100 Companies to Watch for Remote Jobs in 2023! Nearly every company participating tomorrow was featured, and so you'll get access to some great remote-forward employers. Read on to find out more.

As always, thank you for visiting FlexJobs, the best, most trusted remote and hybrid job site available anywhere. We hope you join our premium membership for full access to our job database and the upcoming job fair to give yourself a leg up. And use the special promo code JOB FAIR to save up to 50 percent!

Our Virtual Job Fair is Tomorrow - Are You Registered?

Join us for tomorrow's special job fair from 12:00 p.m. to 4:00 p.m. EST! This is a great opportunity to connect with companies currently hiring, like Outliant, BELAY, UnitedHealth Group, Vista, and TTEC, to name a few.

They will be meeting and interacting with our members, sharing information about job openings, and collecting resumes.

This is a members-only event, so be sure to join FlexJobs today! Use promo code JOB FAIR to save up to 50 percent. This offer expires tomorrow, 1/26/2023.

Learn more about the Virtual Job Fair - sign up and register here.

Thirty Companies Hiring for Part-Time, Remote Jobs

Recently, we analyzed online part-time job postings from our database and identified companies that frequently hire for part-time, remote, work-from-home jobs. Check out this updated list.

What's more important: having the right job title or being able to showcase a diverse set of skills Each approach has pros and cons, so let's look at how to balance your skills and your job title.

Because your career affects every aspect of your life, there's no one-size-fits-all answer. However, with careful consideration,

Empowering Everyone's Storms Of Inflation In Life: Make In Shrinkation

you can find a career perfect for all your interests, needs, and responsibilities.

Job Search Resources

Job Boards and Career Websites

- Zip Recruiter
- Upwork
- Careers.fedex.com/office
- Indeed.com
- Upwork.com
- ziprecruiter.com
- Work.com
- www.idealist.org
- www.unitednations.org
- www.hotjobs.com
- https://my.usajobs.gov
- www.headhunters.com
- www.employmentguide.com

Transportation and Logistics Companies

- Local Transportation Companies
- Sunrise (E-Z Pass Customer Service Representative)
- Uber Eats
- GoAirlinkShuttle.com
- Amtrak

Airlines and Aviation

- United Airlines

- United Career
- Spirit Airlines (Go in person at any Spirit Airlines Office for WFS Application)
- Delta Airlines
- United Airlines.com (Careers)
- US Coast Guard

Retail and Customer Service

- Home Depot
- Best Buy
- Spectrum
- CVS
- Walgreens
- Delivery Pharmacy
- National Car Rental
- Enterprise Car Rental
- Triple A

Healthcare and Medical

- HIV Testing Counselor
- Medical Assistant Billing and Coding (www.eMedPrograms.com)
- EMT
- Medical Transporter

Other Potential Employers

- Life Coach
- Elevator Technician
- Air Conditioner Vent Technician

- Trans Union
- Amazon.com/Apply
- FDA (www.fda.gov/jobs)
- Apartment Housing Complex Employee
- Utility Company
- Churches
- Local Gym
- AARP
- Law firms
- Urgent Care

Resources and Lists

- America's Best Large Employers 2024: The Top 100
- 100 Happiest Companies Hiring Remote Workers in 2024

Find More Great Companies Hiring Remote Workers

Looking to be happier and more productive in your career? Our list of companies with the happiest employees is a great place to start, but you can also check out additional lists, like companies embracing permanent remote work and companies with work-from-anywhere jobs.

Plus, you can explore our extensive database of remote and flexible jobs, which is updated with new job postings across 50 career categories every day and features well-known companies offering remote work, such as:

- AARP jobs
- Amazon jobs
- American Express jobs

- Apple jobs
- Blue Cross Blue Shield jobs
- CVS jobs
- Google jobs
- Kelly jobs
- Meta jobs and Facebook jobs
- Microsoft jobs
- Netflix jobs
- Robert Half jobs
- Target jobs
- Working Solutions jobs
- Yelp jobs

Related Companies That Hire for Remote Work

The below lists are also a great place to target companies that hire remote workers. The companies on these lists are known to provide a healthy remote work environment.

- 16 of the World's Best Regarded Companies Hiring for Remote Jobs
- 25 Remote-First Companies Hiring With Great Cultures
- Best 100 Companies for Healthy Lifestyles
- Best 100 Companies for Remote-Friendly Cultures
- CareerBliss 50 Happiest Companies in America
- Glassdoor Employees Choice – Best Place to Work
- Great Places to Work Awards
- Top 100 Ideal Employers

CHAPTER 4

Exclusive Prohibited Gatekeeper

You're staring at the mountain of bills, that ever-growing Everest of financial woes threatening to topple your resolve. The news blares about inflation, groceries cost more than a king's ransom, and that dream vacation feels like a distant memory. You're not alone, soldier. According to a recent study by the Self-Sufficiency Standard Institute (SSTI), a staggering almost 40 percent of American adults report they struggle to make ends meet each month [2]. That's a significant portion of the population facing similar challenges.

Here's the harsh reality: sometimes, helping others has to start with helping ourselves. We can't pour from an empty cup, and financial insecurity can be a heavy burden that weighs us down and hinders our ability to contribute to our communities.

But take heart because we're not powerless. This chapter will shine a light on the "Exclusive Prohibited Gatekeepers" that stand between us and financial security. These gatekeepers are the obstacles that make it difficult to climb the financial ladder and achieve our goals. Let's break down the most common ones:

- **Massive Economic Overprices:** From soaring rent that eats up half your paycheck to inflated grocery bills that leave you wondering where the "affordable" options went, everything seems to be getting more expensive. It feels like a rigged game where we're constantly losing ground.
- **Lack of Driven Income:** Jobs with stagnant wages or limited opportunities for advancement make it incredibly difficult to stay afloat, let alone save for the future. Finding work that offers a living wage and a path for growth can feel like searching for a unicorn.
- **The Changeling of Effectiveness:** Life throws curveballs. Unexpected medical bills, car repairs, or other emergencies can derail even the most carefully crafted financial plan. It's a constant battle to stay ahead, and setbacks can feel like starting from scratch all over again.

Every successful person you admire has faced their own set of gatekeepers. The difference lies in how they choose to confront them. These are just a few of the gatekeepers we face. But by acknowledging these challenges, we can start to develop strategies to overcome them.

Contrary, as we walk down the catastrophic road we face the journey in life. As we try to figure out the challenges we face daily, we sit down in the seat and strap ourselves in a seat. Taking off like a roller coaster, we experience rough stabilities.

Each of us needs extraordinary caring and motivation. Especially a person who possesses an incredible accountability character of dedication not for themselves to diligently sacrifice for others. Occasionally, I pause and say, "Why am I here in life?" A response that is tuned up and figured out the mind-puzzling question. Not me, however; we are here to commingle with others, despite objectives, challenges, and complexities. Learning from one another is essential whether it be consciously or not aware. My theory, which I embrace from Eddie Rodriguez, is "If you learn something, you share it. If you haven't shared it, you learned nothing." Usually, some people who had grown up in an environment like mines boxed their narratives only being in the company of blacks. Fortunately for me, I welcome all cultures and international backgrounds mainly because I learn from people. We are not going to be living in a Utopia Society in which we expect *perfectness*. Every culture has a sprinkle of salt of bad it exists within.

Embrace the challenges of chaos, trouble, or wrongdoing from people. I stress and heighten this cause so we all can be inspired with gratitude and establish joy. For instance, after severe rainy days, we enjoy the sunshine. When you are to the point with your tongue hanging out your head excessively thirsty, you want water. People who drown in negativity try not to accept that behavior. Keep in mind always have a third eye to project the best. Sharing with you what I interjected in the past conversations with people. If you have a credit card or debit card, would you share your pin number with a person who randomly you see? If you were offered $700 to cut off each finger on your hand, would you abide? A person says to you "I need your keys to where you reside to sip on juice. Give me the keys." What would you say? If you say "Hi," you will be given $1,000,000. If you cooperate by wetting your hand with battery acid and putting your fingers in a wall socket that bears 110 watts, would you comply? If you said "No," "You must be crazy," or "Absolutely no," then you should apply this control of a magnet to battles we should not be fighting unnecessarily.

Another imposing opposition proposal interjected. What is our purpose? Why am I am here on earth and in the world?

I am here to be a public servant to serve others and guide those in need. As I climb the ladder of success, a method to share monies with a selective number of those who are in need.

Overall, I welcome criticism; it is to build a foundation of strength in life and a magnitude of success. When I observe animals such as an eagle, she flies high and above the sky, focusing on her target, never flying looking back. If you examine or have possession of a twenty-five-cent coin, you will see the back of the quarter, which is significant.

Never think you are less than a quarter, but as you glance at it, think of yourself high and mighty, soaring and flying over negativity.

Another animal I observed is a turtle. Even so, its neck is tender and delicate. We represent a similarity of being sensitive and, at times, shy or bashful, expediting life. Facing obstacles in various phases, eventually, we learn to toughen up as the turtle's hard shell combat and protect against predators. Our challenges are to maintain hope, faith, and windows of opportunity and open multiple and endless doors of success through our skills, talents, business, and our comfort zone.

Sharing with you Diane, who I met in the store. As I placed my items on the counter, notified her collective maintained a cool and collective demeanor after a customer was rude to her.

I expressed to the man, "Listen up, that is no way to speak nor talk down to her as a female," especially if men insult women in your family, you would be furious. He walked away.

Diana responded to me, and I carried her words of wisdom and credited her. She said, "Insults are taken and not given." I asked her what she implied. The response was always productive in life since we cannot control people's behavior. Rise above high and mighty.

Every one of us is gifted with hidden treasures of knowledge. We represent a tree that flourishes, casting various sizes of tree branches. We are unique mainly because we have various differences and disagreeing likely we do not like. I find it can, at times, depending on the situation, be a useful tool to enhance matters in a successful way.

As we travel by airplane, have you ever thought of the technology that was administrated for success? A simple natural part of nature assisted the wings of the aircraft to fly. Always the gusting winds against the craft assist its engines to take off.

So when you experience the winds in life, it is to push you in another direction. For instance, celebrities such as Oprah Winfred's struggles in life did not allow her to dwell on being a victim. Look at her now financially independent. Sometimes, our sickness or medical conditions can be a stumbling block. When I reflect on the hero who is legally blind, Stevie Wonder: Governor Gregory Wayne Abbott of Texas, even though his life changed.

At the age of twenty-six, he attended the University of Texas and graduated from the law school at Vanderbilt. One day, he was jogging and suffered an injury, and without any warning, a tree from the storm had fallen on him. Unfortunately, the injuries were devastating; surgeons analyzed that his broken spine contained bone fragments. Subsequently, his ribs were fractured, and the kidneys were damaged. As a result, he is paralyzed below the waist and wheelchair-bound. Despite his disability, he is a strong leader.

We all have medical conditions. Some are visible to the eye as we see Gregory Wayne Abbott, who is wheelchair-bound. When I share with you that I am a pioneer in persistence despite generations of high blood pressure. Work-related injuries: I slipped down a flight of stairs on April 15, 2010, and suffered fractions in my spine, hernia disks, and neck injuries. Several years ago, another incident, on March 3, 2019, had walked up the stairs to drop off equipment and was not aware of black ice. Unfortunately, when I slipped on the stairs, I guarded my face to prevent it from being smashed into the glass door. As a result, I injured my right shoulder and had surgery on March 11, 2024, called arthroplasty surgery completed on March 11, 2024. Despite the injuries, I continued to work, and when severe pain attacked, I was forced to rest. My sacrifice is to be extraordinary and an inspiration to others.

As I excel in business and reach a peak of success, as I encourage you to give back my actions will unfold to share, as God blesses me, I am willing to contribute to community organizations and reward others who need a sophisticated jumpstart. When you are successful, ponder and do the same in the sense of helping others who help themselves do not give a handout but a "helping hand." Here are examples that are geared to establishments.

- American Red Cross
- Catholic Diocese
- City University of New York (CUNY)
- Columbia University
- Newark's Beth Israel Hospital
- Newark's University Hospital
- New York Health and Hospitals Gotham Health Gouverneur
- New York University
- Pace University
- Princeton University
- Rutgers The State University
- Universal Church of the Kingdom of God
- University of Illinois

I like the idea the Diana Heyward embraced me with the idea health is wealth. The information she shared with me was her methods to eliminate high blood pressure, and she does not have any more negative attitudes. However, because of her highly natural and organic approach, the progress of the treatment is subjective to your condition. Also, it may *not* be the sole treatment for your condition, so it's always better to get a doctor's opinion.

Usually, I use a metaphor by squeezing a lemon, which is sour and impacts a productive disposition by sweeting with hope and by remaining calm this way, you can make the bitterness of anger become sweet by creating lemonade.

Family is important, whether it be biological or platonic. My mother had all my siblings by the same father. Unfortunately, he spread his seed to other women. I cannot count the number of half-sisters and half-brothers we have. However, my half-sister, Roz Colson, and I continue to communicate. We do not point the fingers of animosity to one another instead; we are here for a purpose to be acquainted with all of our family and to build on success. I give credit to my half-niece, Yolanda Colson, and her husband, who assisted me in FY-2010.

There are biological blood siblings who do not get along with one another; instead, some of us have associates who are adopted in the place of our family. Sometimes, others are more supportive than our own. Nevertheless, I continue to base my life on peace and harmony. In those areas I cannot control, I take three steps back and dismiss myself from confrontation. This does not mean I am helpless. It is only a trigger point to allow ignorance of people's behavior to sink into a pit hole of destruction.

After many attempts on my end, I try to treat people with respect, and when that is not implied, I utilize by-laws and regulations to combat my protection. In other words, if someone constantly harasses you, there are ways to resolve it. This way, you clear yourself from being placed in a mindset of destruction. Before I act on negativity, I view the consequences and do not entertain the chaos. Of course, we all are human with feelings, and some of us will not back down. However, life taught me once again every battle, you do not have to fight. Keep this thought in mind in life. We are not always going to agree upon the same strategies, and this creates a unique way of using our minds in a productive matter.

Chapter 5

Legal Protections

It's a common human tendency to believe that certain challenges won't happen to us until they do. We often live with a sense of invincibility, assuming that discrimination, harassment, or retaliation are issues that happen to others, not to ourselves. This mindset can leave us ill-prepared and bewildered when faced with such situations unexpectedly.

The good news is you don't have to navigate the financial or even this workplace battlefield alone. New York State law provides a set of legal protections for employees, creating a shield against unfair treatment in the workplace.

As you're going about your workday, focusing on your tasks and goals, you may suddenly find yourself targeted by discrimination or harassment. It's a jarring and disorienting experience that can leave you feeling overwhelmed and unsure of what steps to take or where to turn for help. At that moment, all the theoretical knowledge about laws and rights may seem distant and irrelevant.

Based on my marriage life experience, for eleven and a half years, it was great. However, sharing vital information allows you to decide what is best that works out. Nevertheless, I protected myself with a prenuptial agreement; this protected both of us in case unexpected trauma would surface. Actually, some of us may be excited for marriage, but it is a long-term relationship, even so in the chaotic experiences. Both parties must ask themselves these questions:

A. Do you seriously love another?
B. Are we committed for life?
C. As we grow older, will we still have attraction for each other?
D. Financial challenges with children, who are willing to cope with issues?
E. Financially, are we stable?
F. Do we individually have debt overwhelming that can cause problems?
G. Are we both strong enough not to hold grudges before bed?
H. Do we have methods of communication to put to rest unproductive negativity?
I. Do we love one another regardless of unforeseeable matters?

There might be more questions or uncertainties that need to be processed beforehand. Remember the vow "married for better or worse." Even if we did not have marriage counseling, this may be a remedy for some couples before marriage and during the relationship. Remember, when you have children that are involved, the spouse that earns the highest pay will be responsible for child support and custody may be a battle for one.

In conclusion, prenuptial agreements overall protect both people; if there is refusal, then it is like taking a risk for a future turmoil disaster. Love is not lip service; it is actions!

However, it's important to remember that it's normal to feel unsure and vulnerable when faced with unexpected adversity. It doesn't diminish your worth or your rights. What matters most is how you respond to the challenge and identify what sort of problem it is that you are facing. So you know if the American legal system has a solution to it.

Harassment is a widespread issue that plagues workplaces internationally. Some countries mandate anti-harassment training for all employees, including managers and supervisors. While the specifics of behavior considered harassment can vary, the core concept remains the same: unwelcome conduct that creates a hostile work environment or interferes with job performance. Here's a breakdown by category:

- **Discrimination:** Similar to New York law, many countries have legislation prohibiting discrimination based on race, ethnicity, religion, gender, sexual orientation, disability, and other factors. International Labor Organization (ILO) conventions promote these principles.

- **Bullying:** Unwanted aggressive behavior that can be verbal, physical, psychological, or social. Many countries have laws or regulations addressing bullying, though the specifics may differ.
- **Sexual Harassment:** Unwelcome sexual advances, requests for sexual favors, and other verbal or physical conduct of a sexual nature. The International Labor Organization (ILO) has adopted a convention specifically on sexual harassment at work (Convention 190).

Legal Routes

- **National Laws:** Most countries have national laws addressing workplace harassment. These laws will detail the types of harassment prohibited, the procedures for filing complaints, and potential remedies for victims.
- **International Law:** The International Labor Organization (ILO) sets international standards for workplace harassment through conventions and recommendations. While not directly enforceable, these instruments influence national laws.
- **Company Policies:** Many companies have internal policies that define harassment and outline procedures for employees to report incidents.

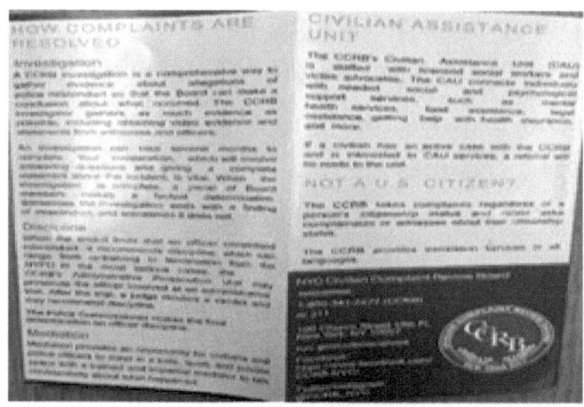

Challenges and Considerations

- **Variations in Laws:** The strength and enforcement of harassment laws can differ significantly between countries.
- **Cultural Differences:** What constitutes harassment can vary based on cultural norms.
- **Difficulty in Reporting:** Fear of retaliation, social stigma, or lack of trust in the system can prevent victims from reporting.

Even if your specific location lacks robust harassment laws, companies often have internal policies. Additionally, international organizations like the ILO promote fair treatment in workplaces globally. Many countries are launching awareness campaigns to educate employees and employers about harassment, its forms, and how to prevent it.

Establish a boundary with people who micromanage your abilities in life, even if it means being patient while navigating through abusive use of the legal system.

Also, for the people who work but are not able to keep insurance coverage, especially those who may get ill for the short or long term, let me introduce you to the options that you can inquire with Mutual Omaha Company. It can easily be found out if a policy works in a person's favor. Do check out

Mutual Omaha Company
https://www.mutualofomaha.com/life-insurance
(800) 228-7104

Chapter 6

Recognition

In the pursuit of financial security, we often focus solely on numbers and strategies, overlooking the profound impact of human connection and support. Every journey has its supporters, and this book, my life, my own journey, is no different. There are people who have inspired me, challenged me, and believed in me throughout my life's path. Here, I want to take a moment to acknowledge a few of those individuals:

- **Church Marines Temple Former Pastor Dr. Henrietta Carter, Dr. Wanda Brown, and Dr. Olene Yarborough:** These remarkable women are not just accomplished professionals but pioneers in their respective fields. They have shattered glass ceilings and paved the way for future generations of women in medicine. Their dedication to their patients and their commitment to excellence inspire me to reach for my own goals and to contribute positively to the world.
- **Michele Fields-Witherspoon Mitchell:** Your dynamic quote of *P*s are "Proper Preparation Prevents Poor Performance," perfectly encapsulating the importance of being prepared to face challenges. This motto resonates deeply with me, not just in academic and

professional pursuits but also in navigating the complexities of personal finance. By taking the time to educate ourselves, research our options, and plan for the future, we can significantly increase our chances of success.
- My best friend **Eddie Rodriguez** and his family members, including his two children—daughter, Jasmine Rodriguez, and son, Joshua Rodriguez—plus his two sisters, Lilly Rodriguez and Tammy Rodriguez. Eddie's quote is a special inspirational word of wisdom he shared with me: "If you learned something, you share it. If you haven't shared it, you learned nothing." Eddie, your belief in the power of knowledge-sharing is a core principle of this book. You understand that financial literacy empowers individuals and strengthens communities.
- Aspirations that I have for Lovejoy Modeste contribute mission is to be a divine representative of Jesus Christ in having love and compassion for others.
- A great person who I truly adore is a friend of mine. Ruth Marisol Ramirez Romero, a life coach who has interactions with people, wholeheartedly is caring. Sharing with you her experiences and background.

Ruth Marisol Ramirez Romero Background

A great person whom I truly adore is a friend of mine. Ruth Marisol Ramirez Romero is a life coach who has interactions with people and is wholeheartedly caring. Sharing with you her experiences and background.

Simply me or we, what do I mean by us? As in the cells within this body; as in protons, electrons within this energetic field this could be we; as in something external, like the chair, like the window, or like you who is reading these words.

Hi, my name is Ruth Marisol Ramirez Romero, a beacon of light for self through the reflection of others. What do I mean by this? I am a beacon of light for self, I am divine, I am abundant. Through the reflection of others when I see you when I hear you, I can see your pain through my past experiences, and since I've healed, then I'm able to recognize something outside of me with compassion and authenticity.

With my light, I intend to shine love or whatever it is that is calling for me to provide for you in a genuine way, and at the same time, if there is a part of me that needs attention or love, then your reflection helps me see that. This reflection helps me give love to me, so thank you infinitely for that.

I am a trajectory of wealth—of knowledge—through various forms. Various experiences: volunteered from a very young age in elementary school with the American Red Cross, volunteered at church fundraisers throughout childhood into teenage years, and volunteered to learn different healing modalities like art therapy, music therapy, and plant medicine through the wounds of others. What does this mean?

I thought that through the wounds that others had given me, I had healed. Little did I know, it was the self-wounds through what I thought others had done to me. This was the medicine that I needed in order for me to move on and heal.

Volunteered for multiple years at the Methodist Hospital in Houston, Texas. And I'm grateful that I had the opportunity, the privilege, and the honor to work side by side with some of the most intelligent and compassionate human beings. I learned so much through these years of volunteering at the Methodist Hospital. In addition, for a brief time, I was a volunteer at the United States Naval Hospital in Camp Lejeune: here I learned to assist and care for cancer patients. This was a beautiful, unique experience. I also worked in the IT Department: an opportunity to learn so much about technology, logistics, and different aspects of customer service or consulting. Later this helped me with many technological experiences, to better prepare, to articulate, to assist, and so much more—I'm so grateful for this.

Furthermore, I volunteered for the deaf community and assisted for multiple years at senior citizen homes: they taught me so much. I engaged in so many meaningful conversations that helped me build and construct a blueprint of what now I'm trying to create for the foundation, the agency, and the vision that I have had since I was two years old.

Counseled many adults, many teenagers, and many children throughout a lifetime. I am very grateful to embrace the now to reflect on the now. By me being part of the now, everything exists in this very moment. My breath, my existence—everything.

Everything because everything exists in the now. Eckhart Tolle talks about this. I exist in the now; unity exists for all. Thank you so much, richest blessings to all for all.

Genuinely authentic I like to recognize Richard Grande who retired on August 7, 2024 after working over 30 years as a Union Lead Shop Stewart with over 100 workers. In addition, he is certified in the field as of Ocean Safety; AED/CPR/First Aid Instructor 18 years taught at the prison system finds it rewarding. Authorized Distributor for Terra Medicus Inc. for FDA approved Automatic External Defibrillators (AED). He volunteers at a Senior Center enjoy assisting people. Still active with the Union involved working with a record store; blues club; he has a passion for music meeting people globally.

Set a trend which I admire Jeanette Cruz recommends Vacation Properties as profits.

Both are extremely patient and work with you. In the event you have renovations in your residence or business, you are welcome to contact them and view their website. Just mentioned that you were referred by Colson.

Beyond these individuals, I am incredibly grateful for the unwavering support of my family members.

My mother, Annie Colson, raising nine children, struggled on welfare and gave me the incentive to work and not rely on public assistance. Even though my father was abusive to the entire family. His mother, Ollie B. Leach, my grandmother, took me under her wing. At the age of four years old, she taught me to spell all entire fifty states here. As a Christian woman, she influenced me also to work. She encourages me to take up typing. Back then, we had manual typewriters, which you said, "Glenn, you are going to need it if you attend college."

I was reluctant, but I noticed when I did learn the keyboard. Never forgot my teacher, Mrs. Brown, who was a black belt in martial arts. She forced me to type without looking at the keyboard. Each time I typed the wrong key, she took a ruler and smashed my fingers over and over again. She dared me to complain and discipline me to the point this gave me wings to work in the clerical field. I had worked shortly at the State of Rutgers University, University Hospital in Newark, New Jersey.

Empowering Everyone's Storms Of Inflation In Life: Make In Shrinkation

To excel in making more income in the City of New York as a clerical associate and office associate, you must pass a typing test in order to be hired. Worked with the New York City Police Department as an office associate and clerical associate I and clerical associate II.

Of course, I was able to pass the minimum test of thirty-five words per minute; approximately five errors were accepted. Now, without looking at the keyboard, I type 120 words per minute.

This had me affiliated with Miracle Temple in Newark, which enforced my methods of trying to do right. For instance, no offense to my viewers, but living in the ghetto, everyone was forced to smoke cigarettes, smoke marijuana, drink alcohol, get involved with gangs, steal cars, and go on the road and spin the vehicles in the shape of donuts, disregarding life; produce children; and sometimes it was a way of being rewarded by the government through receiving welfare or child support, depending on the male's income.

Since, I never once drank alcohol, engaged in taking drugs or selling drugs, or robbed people's apartments while they were at work. In exchange, I encountered bullying and fighting to protect not only myself but my younger siblings. I had a guy named Jamaican John who pulled a knife out on my brother Donald and, all of a sudden, plugged the knife he attempted in his chest. I automatically pushed my brother and was stabbed and fought him from the top of the stairs to the bottom of the staircase. I was not aware of my stabbing because at the age of fourteen years old, fighting a man who was thirty-six years old, known as a drug dealer. A neighbor grabbed me, put me in her apartment, and called the police department, where he was then arrested. As a matter of fact, I later on discovered he was a drug dealer. After I returned from the hospital, the prosecutor took my complaint through my mother since I was a minor. Later on, he tried to correct me to drop the charges. It was beyond my control since the State of New Jersey already proceeded.

The support of these amazing people has played a significant role in shaping who I am today. As you set out on your own quest for financial empowerment, pause to acknowledge and express gratitude to these unsung heroes who have illuminated your path. Recognize the sacrifices they've made, the wisdom they've imparted, and the steadfast support they've provided. In doing so, you not only honor their contributions but also reaffirm the bonds that sustain and enrich your journey.

Article Références

https://youtu.be/zUwKdtXqTp4?si=53oiy2wCIswBFgs-
Interesting Engineering on UVeye – The MRI for Cars

https://youtu.be/bb9g9mtDHZo?si=6N-JkCF_YL8e7i_P
How to Beat Fear and Anxiety (04.25.24)

https://youtu.be/gNfCeDjE9xI?si=QtNud2TDfhBUBT6v
Be Patient to Start Small While Thinking Big - Vusi Thembekwayo

https://youtu.be/bdpO_zWEYxU?si=xGlfiIlmzLk52n5Y
Phantom Debt
Growing strong in the United States. The fashion to buy now and pay later.

Empowering Everyone's Storms Of Inflation In Life: Make In Shrinkation

https://youtu.be/8BfuNrhrv_I?si=-0hayi8iJTNAYaAS
Janie Deegan, she was a drug addicted, and now she own 3 bakeries in New York.
Her statement I liked was "Don't quit before the miracle."

https://youtu.be/R6PGrTFrFzQ?si=Q5HMbn3peLj9vfcu
Dr. Wayne Dyer
Wayne Dyer - Relax and You Will Manifest Anything You Desire.
 Volunteers of America great resources for a people's safety of abuse. Such as:

- Constant headaches
- Anxiety
- Non signs of abuse
- Depression

Contact information available 24 hours per day and 7 days weekly.

Volunteers of America
(855) 643-RISE
7473
Website
voa-gny.org/dv

Another source of income would be the storage business.

Berk Trade School ACCSC / Family Owned and Operated Since 1945
Electrical
Plumbing
718.729.0909

Financial Aid for those who qualify
Job Placement Assistance
Veteran Friendly

ACCSC stands for **Accrediting Commission of Career Schools and Colleges**, a private, nonprofit organization that accredits private post-secondary educational institutions in the United States. The U.S. Department of Education recognizes ACCSC as an independent accrediting agency for over 650 trade and technical schools, as well as postsecondary institutions that offer degrees or distance education programs.

Families in a Rural Texas Town Adopted Seventy-Seven Children This Couple Led the Way

Sound of Hope: The Story of Possum Trot is drawn from the experiences of church leaders Bishop W. C. Martin (Demetrius Grosse) and his wife, Donna (Nika King), who persuaded their rural congregation to adopt more than seventy foster children.

Empowering Everyone's Storms Of Inflation In Life: Make In Shrinkation

August 20, 2012, last updated at 11:29 ET

US Woman Diana Nyad Attempts Cuba to Florida Swim

Nyad has set off on her record attempt without a shark cage

- US woman abandons Cuba to US swim
- "Elusive dream" of Cuba-US swim Watch

A sixty-two-year-old American woman is making good progress on her latest attempt to become the first person to swim from Cuba to the US *without the protection of a shark cage*, her support team says.

Diana Nyad suffered several jellyfish stings and hit storms, but is continuing her 166 km. (103 mile) swim.

She left the Cuban capital, Havana, on Saturday and aims to reach Florida on Tuesday, the day before she turns sixty-three.

She is relying on an electronic shield as a shark deterrent.

It is her fourth attempt. Nyad first attempted the swim in 1978.

Her second attempt was cut short by shoulder pain and an asthma attack.

And the long-distance swimmer was forced to abort her most recent attempt last September after potentially deadly jellyfish stings.

She had to bring the latest attempt forward by sixteen hours because of bad weather.

Man with Golden Voice, Ted Williams, One Year after Shooting to Fame

By Jordan Chittley | <u>Daily Buzz</u> – Thursday, January 12, 2012

Empowering Everyone's Storms Of Inflation In Life: Make In Shrinkation

Just over a year ago (1.6.11) when the world first saw Ted Williams, he was homeless and standing at the side of a road holding a sign that said he had a great voice.

Now the man with the golden voice has a much different look. He has a clean haircut, glasses, is no longer wearing a camouflage jacket, and is living under a roof.

Williams shot to fame after the Columbus Dispatch newspaper posted a <u>video</u> shot by Doral Chenoweth. Williams was standing at the side of a road with a sign that read, "I have a God-given gift of voice." Curious, Chenoweth asked Williams to say something and the video took off.

<u>Chenoweth caught up with Williams</u> at the end of last month and said he has completed a three-month drug rehabilitation program, is off the streets, and is working. He is living just outside Columbus, Ohio, in Dublin and is doing voice-overs for a Boston-based cable network.

The TV show *Entertainment Tonight* also met up with Williams as he celebrated a year after his video went viral.

"A year ago today I was living in tents under bridges, smoking crack, doing all the wild things," he said in the <u>video</u>. Now he has a fireplace, a flat-screen TV, and a walk-in closet that doubles as a recording studio.

"What a difference a year makes," he said as he admits to not being able to dream of living in a spacious home more than a year ago. "It's a halleluiah moment every day I wake up."

But it hasn't been an easy year for Williams as he shot to fame.

Shortly after the video went viral, the Ohio paper that posted the video was inundated with calls and emails offering Williams opportunities. The <u>Cleveland Cavaliers offered him</u>

a full-time job doing voice-over work and offered to pay the mortgage on a home. He also made the rounds on national morning shows including one where he reunited with his mother.

However, the quick fame appeared to be too much for Williams to handle.

Less than a week after the video went viral, he was detained by police in Hollywood after being involved in a verbal altercation with his daughter in a hotel room. They were staying at the hotel prior to an appearance on the *Dr. Phil* show. Williams reunited with his ex-wife and five of his nine children on the show.

The day after the *Dr. Phil* show announced Williams was heading to rehab. "(Williams) agreed to go to a private facility following a lengthy one-on-one conversation with Dr. Phil," read a statement issued by the show.

"I've told him it's not going to be easy and it's going to take a lot of hard work," said Dr. Phil in the statement in an <u>Access Hollywood</u> article. "It might be a long journey for him, but this is a big step in the right direction."

In the twenty years prior to becoming an overnight Internet sensation, Williams had been charged with robbery, escape, forgery, and drug possession.

Now, both Chenoweth and ET report Williams is sober and doing much better.

His book titled *A Golden Voice: How Faith, Hard Work, and Humility Brought Me from the Streets to Salvation* is set to be released in May.

Man with Golden Voice, Ted Williams, One Year after Shooting to Fame

By Jordan Chittley | [Daily Buzz](#) – Thursday, Jan. 12, 2012

Ted Williams holds a sign advertising his smooth radio voice near a highway ramp in Columbus, Ohio, in 2010 (Photo: Doral Chenoweth III, AP). In January 2011, homeless and broke Ted Williams stood in the cold at a busy intersection in Columbus, Ohio, hoping for a miracle.

In the twenty years prior to becoming an overnight Internet sensation, Williams had been charged with robbery, escape, forgery and drug possession. The former radio announcer was trying to piece his life back together after it was ravaged by drugs and alcohol.

"My family had all given up on me," Williams told NBC News in an interview this week. Williams's chance to start over came when *Columbus Dispatch* reporter noticed his sign, which pleaded for help and boasted about Williams's "God-given gift of voice."

I have never been more impressed and inspired by anyone in my life as I have been from you. I rate the opportunity to meet and hear you speak as one of the top ten moments of my life so far (Venki Prathivadi, *Head of Australia & New Zealand for Mahindra Satyam*).

Who Is Jessica Cox?

Jessica is recognized internationally as an inspirational keynote speaker. Born without arms, Jessica now flies airplanes, drives cars, and otherwise lives a normal life, using her feet as others use their hands. She holds the title of the first person without arms in the American Taekwondo Association to get a black belt and the Guinness World Record for being the first armless person in aviation history to earn a pilot's certificate. Convinced that the way we think has a greater impact on our lives than our physical constraints, she chose to pursue a degree in psychology at the University of Arizona. Since then, she has traveled to seventeen countries, sharing her inspirational message.

If Jessica can fly a plane with only her feet, what can you do?

Armless Girl Jessica Cox Gains Pilot's License

Summary

Email forward tells the inspirational story of Jessica Cox, a girl who was able to gain her pilot's license, among other remarkable achievements, in spite of being born without arms **(Full commentary below)**.

Status
True

Example (Submitted on January 2008)
Subject: FW: Armless Girl Gets a Pilot License

Jessica Cox, twenty-five, a girl born without arms, stands inside an aircraft. The girl from Tucson, Arizona, got the Sport Pilot certificate lately and became the first pilot licensed to fly using only her feet.

Glenn Colson

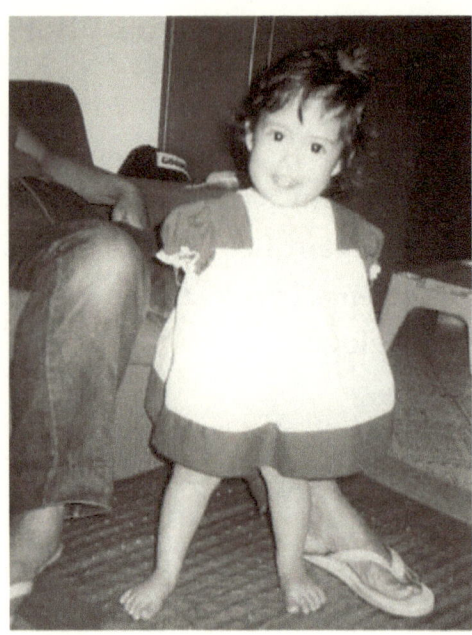

Jessica Cox of Tucson was born without arms, but that has only stopped her from doing one thing: using the word *can't*.

Empowering Everyone's Storms Of Inflation In Life: Make In Shrinkation

Her latest flight into the seemingly impossible is becoming the first pilot licensed to fly using only her feet.

With one foot manning the controls and the other delicately guiding the steering column, Cox, twenty-five, soared to achieve a Sport Pilot certificate. Her certificate qualifies her to fly a light-sport aircraft to altitudes of 10,000 feet.

Glenn Colson

First Armless Pilot

Meet your new hero.

Courtesy of Jessica Cox

By Kenny Thapoung
Aug. 27, 2015

"She's a good pilot. She's rock solid," said Parrish Traweek, forty-two, the flying instructor at San Manuel's Ray Blair Airport.

Parrish Traweek runs PC Aircraft Maintenance and Flight Services and has trained many pilots, some of whom didn't come close to Cox's abilities.

"When she came up here driving a car," Traweek recalled, "I knew she'd have no problem flying a plane."

Doctors never learned why she was born without arms, but she figured out early on that she didn't want to use prosthetic devices.

The first thing you'll notice about Jessica Cox, thirty-two, is that she has no arms. It's okay—she's used to the stares. But when you actually talk to the first—as in, like, *ever*—armless pilot and black belt, you learn that her arms don't define who she is.

Cox has lived with her condition since birth with no explanation as to why she was born without what most of us view as essential appendages. But *c'est la vie* because this is all Cox has known her entire life, and she's adapted quite nicely to her surroundings—she can fly planes, for goodness sake. And when she's not attacking a punching bag with her heels or finishing her documentary Right Footed, Cox makes her living as a motivational speaker. After you hear her backstory, you'll understand why everyone finds her so inspiring—we guarantee it.

Jessica Cox: It bothered me a little because I was so insistent on finding an answer. Most children are curious about what makes them how they are. I went to my mom and asked, "Why am I different? I have so many people around me with arms." From what I saw, I was the only one who didn't have them.

It was a devastating time—especially for my mom. My parents had no idea I was going to be born with a birth defect. She actually had a normal pregnancy and she was excited I was going to be her first girl. Most of the time, it's more [shocking] for the parents than the kid because the child doesn't know anything different. This is my normal and I've grown up to accept it.

MC: Did you opt for prosthetic arms at all?

JC: I wore them for eleven years. They became part of my everyday routine: I would put them on just like a jacket (or football equipment) and go to school. I was very patient with them and therapy, but I didn't like them. My mom knew I didn't like wearing them, but she heard from the specialist that I needed to grow into [the prosthetics] while I was young. Doctors would say that if I didn't learn to use them while I was younger, there was no chance I'd be able to use them as an adult. They had to make sure the option was available to me.

Come eighth grade—age fourteen—I got rid of them.

MC: Why did you ultimately decide to give them up?

JC: It's hard for me to explain this to someone with arms—you can't imagine anything different. Because I was born this way, [everything] felt more natural to do with my feet. Plus, there's nothing like the sensation of feeling things with flesh and bone. Prosthetics just felt very foreign to me: You wear them on your shoulders, strap them to your chest, and they're heavy and uncomfortable. If someone gave you a hug, you'd miss that touch. They were more like a cage for me.

MC: I watched this video of you playing the piano, eating with chopsticks, typing on a keyboard—all with your feet. Just how did you train yourself to do all these seemingly "normal" things?

JC: I don't look at it as training—it's more like adapting as would a three-year-old learning to trace letters in a preschool class. Just as anyone learns through their childhood during their stages of development, I went through the normal stages. There was a bit of a delay learning how to crawl [and walk] because most toddlers use their arms to grab furniture to pull themselves up. I went through therapy to learn how to walk, and I probably started [walking] two to three months later than the average toddler.

MC: What about dressing yourself?

JC: Oh yes. Getting dressed is quite the process—I always say that's the most difficult physical task for someone without arms. Getting a shirt on wasn't a big deal, but getting pants and underwear on was more of a process as a kid. I went through ten or eleven years of figuring out what system would work. I use a hook that suctions on the wall, like the ones on doors to hang clothes except lower on the wall so that I could wiggle my way into my pants. The suction cup allows me to take it everywhere I go.

MC: Basically, you kick ass at life—and physically as a black belt. Why did you want to start practicing taekwondo?

JC: When I was ten, my mom enrolled me and my brother and sister in taekwondo because she thought it'd be a phenomenal way to have us do something together as a family. Also, I tended to take out my anger and frustration in kicks—and unfortunately, my siblings were the targets. My mom had to put me into something that would channel [my emotions] in a very positive way, and according to my brother, it really did help.

Empowering Everyone's Storms Of Inflation In Life: Make In Shrinkation

I had envisioned myself getting that black belt, and four years later I got my first one in the International Taekwon-Do Federation. I stopped for a while and picked it up again in college. I rejoined a school and club and earned my second black belt in [American Taekwondo Association (ATA)]. I've been practicing since that sophomore year in college back in 2002 and I am now a third-degree black belt in the ATA.

Courtesy of Jessica Cox

MC: So now I know never to pick a fight with you. What about being the first person without arms to fly a plane? You have to admit that's pretty awesome.

JC: If you would've asked me about getting a pilot's license before 2005, I'd say you were crazy. After I graduated college, a fighter pilot asked me if I wanted to go up on a flight in a single-engine plane. I always had a fear about being in an airplane, but I took this opportunity to go up on my first flight in a single-engine rather than a big commercial plane I was accustomed to. I was hooked and made a commitment to become a pilot. I wanted to motivate others to not let fear stand in the way of their opportunities.

MC: What exactly were you so afraid of though?

JC: Well, it was losing contact with the ground—not heights. I've always been a daredevil—I loved climbing and looking down from new heights. But maybe it was that lack of control you have [when you're in the air]. I shortly learned that if you can fly an airplane competently, you can fly it safely even if something does happen.

MC: On your website, it says, "It took three states, four airplanes, two flight instructors, and a discouraging year to find the right aircraft." Why did it take so long?

JC: Not only was it an emotional fear, which didn't stop me, but it was more of a logistical challenge. Airplanes are not designed to be flown with your feet. I fly an Ercoupe—it's the only one that doesn't have rudder pedals—and it's *not* an airplane that's been modified by me—it wasn't specially built for me.

It's a standard Ercoupe that's seventy-five years old. It worked out that this was my fit. Because it was so old, it took an in-depth search to find *this* type of plane. It needed to be owned by someone—eventually I found Parrish Traweek—who'd train me but also who had insurance to allow me to be one of their students.

MC: What's it like to actually be in the air?

JC: That takeoff isn't scary at all—just the landing. Once you're in the air, you feel that sense of freedom of no limits.

Kidnapped Eighty-Nine-Year-Old Has a Message for Her Captors

12:18 PM, Apr. 7, 2013 | 0 comments

Photo: Margaret Smith (courtesy of ABC News)

(ABC NEWS)—An eighty-nine-year-old woman who spent two days locked in her car trunk, thinking she'd never be found, has a message for her teen captors.

"You got to be kind to other people if you want somebody to be kind to you," Margaret Smith said.

The four-foot-eleven octogenarian's story began with an act of kindness on March 18.

Smith had stopped at the Chicken Man Convenience Store in Milford, Del., for a butter pecan ice cream cone when two teenage girls approached her and asked for a ride across town.

"I decided not to, then I said, 'Well, a good deed,'" Smith said.

After driving around for a while, Smith said the girls snatched her car keys and stuffed her in the trunk of her Buick.

"The way they drove off flying, I didn't think nobody would ever find me," she said. "I just had to pray about and hope that I'd be found."

Smith spent the next two days crammed in the trunk, without food, water, and her blood pressure medication. She said the only time the girls opened the trunk was to rob her of the cash she was carrying.

"I was very tired, cold, hungry, scared," Smith said. "I didn't know what to expect."

After spending forty-eight hours locked in her trunk, Smith's kidnappers inexplicably decided to dump her in a remote cemetery.

"I was crawling through the cemetery on hands and knees," Smith said. "Nothing but a pair of stockings on, no jacket . . . Finally somebody found me. I don't know who."

Smith was taken to a local hospital, where her family, who had reported her missing, received a call that she was safe.

Delaware State Police found Smith's car days later and arrested and charged five teenagers inside. All are believed to have some involvement in the kidnapping, robbery, and theft, ABC News's Philadelphia affiliate WPVI reported.

Four of the teens, ranging in age from fourteen to seventeen, are being charged as adults while a fifth faces receiving stolen property and conspiracy charges as a minor.

ABC News

Empowering Everyone's Storms Of Inflation In Life: Make In Shrinkation

September 2, 2013, last updated at 18:24 ET

US Swimmer Diana Nyad, Sixty-Four, Makes Cuba-Florida Crossing

Diana Nyad: "You are never too old to chase your dreams."

Endurance swimmer Diana Nyad has become the first person to swim from Cuba to the US without a shark cage.

After about fifty-three hours' nonstop swimming, the sixty-four-year-old American reached Key West, Florida, escorted by boats and her team of thirty-five people.

Ms. Nyad, who left a Havana yacht club early on Saturday, had vowed this would be her last attempt to cross the 110-mile (177 km.) wide Florida Straits.

Her four other tries—one in 1978, two in 2011, and one in 2012—failed.

Ms. Nyad walked out of the water on to the beach just before 14:00 local time (18:00 GMT) on Monday.

"Lifelong Dream"

A couple of hundred well-wishers were waiting to greet her on the beach, cheering and blowing horns.

The breathless athlete told waiting TV crews: "I have three messages: one is we should never ever give up, two is you are never too old to chase your dreams, and three is it looks like a solitary sport but it is a team."

Before her swim, Ms. Nyad had said she was more worried about jellyfish than sharks. Last year, she was forced to halt an attempt after being badly stung by box jellyfish.

"I have to say," Ms. Nyad added, "I'm a little bit out of it right now."

As well as a bodysuit, gloves, and booties, she wore a special silicone mask to protect her face from the jellyfish stings that plagued her last attempt.

She acknowledged beforehand that the kit would slow her down, but believed it would ultimately prove effective.

Ms. Nyad's support team had equipment that generated a faint electrical field around her, which was designed to keep sharks at bay.

US President Barack Obama congratulated her, tweeting: "Never give up on your dreams."

As she prepared for the home stretch, Ms. Nyad stopped swimming briefly to address her support team, according to a blog post on her website.

"I am about to swim my last two miles in the ocean," she said. "This is a lifelong dream of mine and I'm very, very glad to be with you."

Medics had concerns about her slurred speech and breathing, but they did not intervene, according to her website.

Ms. Nyad's team guided her through the best route into Key West to avoid dangerous eddies, currents, shipping lanes, reefs, and swarms of jellyfish.

The rules of the swim meant she was not allowed to hold on to the support boat at any time. Her team helped to keep her on course and gave her food and water.

During her last attempt in August 2012, Ms. Nyad had to be pulled out of the water after forty-one hours when a squall and repeated jellyfish stings made it impossible for her to continue.

She first tried to complete the crossing in 1978 with a shark cage.

A second attempt - without a cage - in 2011 had to be called off because of shoulder pain and an asthma attack.

Later the same year, jellyfish stings stopped Ms. Nyad's third bid at the crossing. Her fourth attempt ended in August 2012.

Australian Susie Maroney, who was twenty-two at the time, successfully swam the Straits in 1997 with a shark cage.

Besides the protection it affords from predators, the structure is said to make the swim itself easier as it creates a drafting effect. Gliding on ocean currents, the cage enabled Ms. Maroney to make the journey in just twenty-five hours. In June, Australian endurance swimmer Chloe McCardel tried to make the crossing without a shark cage, but had to give up because of jellyfish stings.

Glenn Colson

August 20, 2012, last updated at 11:29 ET

Sixty-three-year old woman attempts to swim from Cuba to Florida, makes it halfway before quitting.

Donations for Honest Homeless Man Tops $100K

Sept. 19, 2013
By Christina Ng
Christina Ng More from Christina"

via Good Morning America
Share on email
7 Comments

Empowering Everyone's Storms Of Inflation In Life: Make In Shrinkation

Glen James at a news conference at police headquarters, in Boston, Sept. 16, 2013.
Steven Senne/AP Photo

Fundraising for a Boston homeless man heralded as an honest guy after handing in a backpack he found that contained over $40,000 in cash and travelers checks has topped more than $104,000 in just a few days.

"I'm in complete shock," Ethan Whittington, the man who organized the fundraiser, told ABCNews.com today with a laugh. "It's more money than I've ever seen."

"It's completely changing my life," he said. "It gets you thinking. Imagine the possibilities if we continue to do this as a nation. It's so inspiring to see the way that everyone is coming together."

The money has been raised by more than 4,000 strangers since the campaign was posted on GoFundMe.com on Monday. Donations and messages have poured in from all over the US as well as countries as far as Brazil, France and Australia.

Whittington has set the effort's fundraising goal at $250,000. "There's no mathematical equation on why I did that," he said of the quarter of a million dollar amount. "I just want to see what we can do."

Glen James found the black backpack with $2,400 in cash, $39,500 in travelers checks and a passport at the South Bay Mall in Dorchester on Saturday evening. He promptly reported it to police.

Officers then returned the bag to the owner, a student visiting from China, and Boston Police Commissioner Ed Davis presented a special citation to James for his "extraordinary show of character and honesty." The fundraising campaign began when Whittington heard about what James had done, but it didn't mention James getting anything other than a plaque.

"Beautiful! I pray that he is blessed beyond measure for his act of integrity and kindness," one woman wrote on the GoFundMe page. "We could all take a lesson from him. Someone help him invest wisely and all will be well!"

"Nicest idea I can think of for a man who deserves this miracle," another person wrote.

Many people have contacted Whittington about James and expressed interest in doing this for him including donating computers to James, providing him dental care and helping him find a job.

Whittington last spoke to James on Tuesday when the donation amount was at $15,000 and James was "ecstatic," he said.

Whittington suggested to James the possibility of someone to help him with handling the money when he gets it.

"I want to be very careful about how we go about doing it," Whittington said. "It's a lot of money. If someone came up to me and handed me a hundred grand, I wouldn't know what the hell to do with it."

"I want this to come out to be a positive influence for his life, not for it to be completely out of control and then we have some horror story a couple of months from now," he said. Whittington is planning to travel to Boston to meet James in person and find out more about his life. "I have the best intentions for Glen," he said. "There's only so much I can do. I'm going to give him 150 percent of my effort to do what I can to help him out, but it's his money. I can't make these decisions for him."

Donations for Billy Ray Harris, Kansas City, Missouri, homeless man who returned diamond and platinum engagement ring, approach 180K—and campaign has seventy-one days left!

The national outpouring of support has helped Harris take the first steps toward getting back on his feet. More importantly, he says, the publicity surrounding his good deed has put him back in touch with his family in Texas.

By Philip Caulfield
New York Daily News
Published: Wednesday, March 6, 2013, 9:43 AM
Updated: Wednesday, March 6, 2013, 10:20 AM

A homeless man's sterling character has led him to a pot of gold.

Billy Ray Harris, who weeks ago was sleeping on the streets in Kansas City, Missouri, is set to receive nearly $180,000 from donors as a reward for returning a diamond engagement ring to a woman who mistakenly dropped it in his change cup.

More than 7,700 people have donated to the Give Forward campaign started by Bill Krejci and his wife, Sarah Darling, who thought her treasured ring was lost forever when she dropped it in Harris' cup on Feb. 8.

Harris held onto the ring and returned it to Darling the next day. The couple gave him all the money they had on them—around fifty bucks—and launched the online campaign a few days later, with the goal of raising $1,000.

Empowering Everyone's Storms Of Inflation In Life: Make In Shrinkation

Kidnapped Eighty-Nine-Year-Old's Message to Her Captors: "You Got to Be Kind to Other People"

By Alyssa Newcomb and Gio Benitez | *Good Morning America* – Sun., Apr. 7, 2013 5:38 PM EDT

Good Morning America—Kidnapped Eighty-Nine-Year-Old's Message to Her Captors: "You Got to Be Kind to Other People" (ABC News)

An eighty-nine-year-old woman who spent two days locked in her car trunk, thinking she'd never be found has a message for her teen captors.

The four-foot-eleven octogenarian's story began with an act of kindness on March 18.

Smith had stopped at the Chicken Man Convenience Store in Milford, Del., for a butter pecan ice cream cone when two teenage girls approached her and asked for a ride across town.

"I decided not to, then I said, 'Well, a good deed,'" Smith said.

After driving around for a while, Smith said the girls snatched her car keys and stuffed her in the trunk of her Buick.

"The way they drove off flying, I didn't think nobody would ever find me," she said. "I just had to pray about and hope that I'd be found."

Smith spent the next two days crammed in the trunk, without food, water, and her blood pressure medication. She said the only time the girls opened the trunk was to rob her of the cash she was carrying.

"I was very tired, cold, hungry, scared," Smith said. "I didn't know what to expect."

After spending forty-eight hours locked in her trunk, Smith's kidnappers inexplicably decided to dump her in a remote cemetery.

"I was crawling through the cemetery on hands and knees," Smith said. "Nothing but a pair of stockings on, no jacket . . . Finally somebody found me. I don't know who."

Smith was taken to a local hospital, where her family, who had reported her missing, received a call that she was safe.

"You got to be kind to other people if you want somebody to be kind to you," Margaret Smith said.

Delaware State Police found Smith's car days later and arrested and charged five teenagers inside. All are believed to have some involvement in the kidnapping, robbery, and theft, ABC News' Philadelphia affiliate WPVI reported.

Four of the teens, ranging in age from fourteen to seventeen, are being charged as adults while a fifth faces receiving stolen property and conspiracy charges as a minor.

Glenn Colson

Florida Whiz Kid, Sixteen, Graduates College before High School

Grace Bush received her degree from Florida Atlantic University on Friday with a 3.8 GPA. She will receive her 'other' diploma on Friday as part of the dual-enrollment program.

By David Boroff
New York Daily News
Tuesday, May 6, 2014, 1:00 PM

It's a true Hollywood story.

A sixteen-year-old Florida whiz kid graduated from high school and college in the same week — completing college first.

"It's kind of weird that I graduated college before high school," Grace Bush told CBS in Miami.

Grace, who lives in Hollywood, Florida, received her degree from Florida Atlantic University on Friday with a sparkling 3.8 grade-point average. She will receive her "other" diploma on Friday from Florida Atlantic University high school.

The teen was participating in FAU's special dual-enrollment program, which gives more talented students college credit for selected high school courses.

"I started when I was 13 at Broward College, and I also took my classes throughout the summer, so I was able to finish it before four years," she told CBS.

Grace is just following a family tradition. She is the third oldest of nine children, and her parents would like all their kids to do what Grace did to save tuition. The kids are homeschooled as well.

Sixteen-Year-Old FAU Grad Has Designs on Supreme Court

WPBF - West Palm Beach, FL

Typically a sixteen-year-old is just hoping to get her hands on the car keys. But Grace Bush has slightly bigger plans.

Share on emailPrivacy PolicyTerms of UseShare on email"My two older sisters are doing it, and I'm the third to do it," Grace told CBS. "My oldest sister already graduated, and my second oldest sister is graduating in the summer."

Grace, who was reading at age two, has some ambitious goals.

Denied for Her Disability: How One Makeup Artist Is Defying the Odds

Dec. 4, 2015, at 4:06 PM

Like any makeup artist, Jessica Ruiz prides herself on expertly applied eye shadow, glowing skin, and the ability to transform a face and lift someone's confidence with cosmetics.

But to watch her work is like nothing else—Ruiz suffers from a condition called arthrogryposis, which affects the joints in her limbs, and so she gets around in a wheelchair and has limited use of her hands.

To apply makeup to clients, she holds the brush in between her teeth, stabilizing it with her tongue.

Makeup artist Jessica Ruiz gets to work
on a model in Philadelphia

"At first, they're a little uncomfortable," Ruiz, of Philadelphia, told TODAY.com of the moment new clients discover her unusual technique. "But then they warm up really quickly, and they just want the experience!"

"A lot of times I won't let them know I do makeup with my mouth until I sit down and speak with them," she added. "I won't touch their face until we have a conversation. Trust is key with any makeup artist."

Related: Makeup artist Lisa Eldridge recreates 2,000 years of makeup history on YouTube

But Ruiz's journey hasn't been an easy one. The twenty-six-year-old says she was turned down from cosmetology schools she applied to after high school and initially struggled to find to work because of her condition.

"They denied me because of my disability and the way I apply makeup to my clients," she said. "They told me it was unsanitary, and that no one would want me that close to their face."

"I could probably talk to you for hours about all the disappointments and the hurdles," Ruiz added.

So the self-taught artist struck out on her own, blindly reaching out to designers and fashion shows to see if she could help.

Ruiz's biggest break yet came in October, when she worked for Philadelphia Small Business Fashion Week, after contacting founder Dawane Cromwell.

Related: Madeline Stuart, model with Down syndrome, will walk at NYFW

"I explained to him, 'Listen, I'm not just a makeup artist. I'm a disabled makeup artist, and this is how I do makeup,'" she said. "His reaction, surprisingly, was 'All right, that doesn't matter to me, come in and show me what you can do.'"

"That was the door I really needed," added Ruiz, who works under the name Dreamy Eyes Artistry.

Jessica Ruiz applies makeup with her mouth because she has limited use of her hands.

Cromwell told TODAY.com that if he hesitated at all, it was only to make sure the venue was handicapped-accessible, adding that she did a "fabulous job" that week, doing makeup for more than twenty models.

"I was actually excited to witness it for myself, and the makeup room was the first place I visited when I walked into the venue," he said.

Related: Kylie Jenner's wheelchair photo for Interview magazine cover stirs backlash

Cromwell hired Ruiz to come back as a lead makeup artist next year, for both the small business fashion week as well as Philadelphia Kids Fashion Week, which he also runs. In the meantime, she's working on building her client list, doing about three to four appointments a week, and attending casting calls for other fashion shows.

"As the holidays approach, the calendar is filling up really quickly," she said. "I'm actually getting a little bit nervous, to be honest."

Empowering Everyone's Storms Of Inflation In Life: Make In Shrinkation

Billionaire Warren Buffet Still Lives in Modest Omaha Home He Bought for $31,500 in 1958 (Though He Does Have $4M Californian Home—But Even That Was a Bargain)

Read more: By James Nye

Published: 01:25 EST, 21 January 2013 | Updated: 05:33 EST, 21 January 2013

Even though he is recognized as the world's third richest man with a fortune of $46 billion, investor Warren Buffet, the Wizard of Omaha still lives in the same modest home he bought in 1958 for $31,500.

Despite his wealth giving him almost limitless property options, the famously frugal and modest Buffet, eighty-two, lives in a well-kept gray stucco house in the Dundee-Happy Hollow Historic District of Omaha, Nebraska.

There is no gate, no security guard, and no surveillance cameras protecting the home of one of the most powerful men in the world and was last assessed as being worth $700,000—although the billionaire believes that valuation to be optimistic.

Billionaire Warren Buffett still lives in the same home that he bought for $31,500 in the Dundee-Happy Hollow Historic District of Omaha, Nebraska, where he was raised.

CEO and chairman of Berkshire Hathaway, Buffet runs his multibillion dollar empire from the 6,000 square-foot home which he calls the third best investment he ever made, after the rings he bought for his two wives.

The Oracle of Omaha does not have a portfolio of homes, instead residing in the relative upper-middle class luxury of the home which he purchased for approximately $250,000 in today's dollars.

Empowering Everyone's Storms Of Inflation In Life: Make In Shrinkation

Known for his modest and frugal tastes Warren Buffett (*left*), CEO and chairman of investment company Berkshire Hathaway, attends the twenty-fifth anniversary dinner of the Economic Club of Washington in Washington in June.

The home sits on a corner and was built in 1921 and does appear to have had some additions added over the past fifty-five-years.

However, crucially, the property falls short of the definition of a mansion, which is usually considered to be 10,000 square feet.

According to Realtor.com, the home is valued at $652,619 and a neighboring five-bedroom, six-bathroom, 3,848 square-foot house was put on the market for $450,000.

Indeed, the home is not even the highest valued on the block. Despite being slightly smaller, the house next door is valued by Realtor.com at $826,870.

Asked why he hasn't traded up for a more luxurious home, the billionaire was unequivocal.

It is reported that Warren Buffet also drives a simple unpretentious Lincoln Town car similar to the one pictured here.

"I'm happy there. I'd move if I thought I'd be happier someplace else," he said in a BBC interview two years ago.

"How would I improve my life by having ten houses around the globe? If I wanted to become a superintendent of housing, I could have as a profession, but I don't want to manage ten houses and I don't want somebody else doing it for me and I don't know why the hell I'd be happier.

"I'm warm in the winter, I'm cool in the summer, it's convenient for me," he said in the interview. "I couldn't imagine having a better house."

However, Buffet does have a luxury vacation home in Laguna Beach which he sold in the spring of $4.3 million.

Forbes reports "that's still less than one hundredth of a percent of his estimated net worth."

The house sits on the ocean side of the Pacific Coast Highway on a private cul-de-sac. It has four bedrooms, four baths, and 3,100 square feet.

Empowering Everyone's Storms Of Inflation In Life: Make In Shrinkation

Student Goes from Homeless to Harvard

Posted 5:04 pm, May 31, 2012, by Lorrie Taylor

Cleveland, Ohio—David Boone, eighteen, walks the halls of Cleveland's MC2STEM High School in his navy blue blazer, looking like a young man who owns the world. Chances are good that's the kind of success he will find one day, not only because of where he's going but because of where he's been.

"Childhood is childhood. You live, you learn, and sometimes some challenges are thrown at you," he said.

David was homeless for part of his high school career; his family torn apart he says, by a neighborhood gang that resented his refusal to join.

"I guess their mentality was, 'You're either with us, or you're against us,'" he told Fox 8 News. Eventually, it resulted in them vandalizing my home, making it unlivable."

David's allergies to pets prevented him from living with a family friend where his brothers and sisters were sent. It was the same with his mother's new home. David was left to fend for himself.

"That kind of put me in a position to where like I had to find different places back and forth to stay, and sometimes there was no place to go. I had to make a tough decision: where was I sleeping at night?" he remembered.

Sometimes he slept on a park bench, sometimes he slept nowhere at all, but through it all, he studied science, technology, engineering, and math at MC2STEM, one of Cleveland's new and innovative schools from where he will graduate with a full ride to Harvard University.

"I saw that as the way out. I saw going to any college as the way to escape and a way to secure that these types of things don't continue to happen to my family," said the eighteen-year-old.

He is one of the 1,000 students guaranteed an education through the doctoral level thanks to a Gates Millennium Scholarship, an accomplishment of which he is proud.

I've always had this confident air about myself. I'm very humble, but it's just like I always believe in myself," he told Fox 8 News.

He believes in others too and in setting an example for them to follow. David plans to revisit MC2STEM, when he's home from school, to encourage the kids who will one day claim a diploma as he is about to.

It is a dream born under the stars from a bench that once doubled as a bed.

"For me, I promised myself I wouldn't cry, everyone does before they cry," the teenager laughed. "I'm pretty sure there's going to be a lot of emotion there."

Twenty-two universities, including Harvard and Princeton, accepted David into their programs.

He intends to study electrical engineering and computer science.

Chinese Drone Maker Unveils Human-Carrying Drone

January 6, 2016, by Ryan Nakashima

The EHang 184 autonomous aerial vehicle is unveiled at the EHang booth at CES International, Wednesday, Jan. 6, 2016, in Las Vegas. The drone is large enough to fit a human passenger (AP Photo/John Locher).

Chinese drone maker Ehang Inc. on Wednesday unveiled what it calls the world's first drone capable of carrying a human passenger.

The Guangzhou, China-based company pulled the cloth off the Ehang 184 at the Las Vegas Convention Center during the CES gadget show. In a company video showing it flying, it looks like a small helicopter but with four doubled propellers spinning parallel to the ground like other drones.

The electric-powered drone can be fully charged in two hours, carry up to 220 pounds, and fly for twenty-three minutes at sea level, according to Ehang. The cabin fits one person and a small backpack and even has air conditioning and a reading light. With propellers folded up, it's designed to fit in a single parking spot.

After setting a flight plan, passengers only need to give two commands, "take off" and "land," each controlled by a single click on a Microsoft Surface tablet, the company said.

It is designed to fly about 1,000 to 1,650 feet off the ground with a maximum altitude of 11,500 feet and top speed of sixty-three miles per hour.

US authorities are just starting to lay out guidelines for drone use, and a human-passenger drone seems certain to face strict scrutiny.

The EHang 184 autonomous aerial vehicle is unveiled at the EHang booth at CES International, Wednesday, Jan. 6, 2016, in Las Vegas. The drone is large enough to fit a human passenger (AP Photo/John Locher).

Federal Aviation Administration administrator Michael Huerta was at CES but could not immediately be reached for comment through a spokesman.

Ehang, cofounder, and Shang Hsiao, chief financial officer, said the company hopes to sell the device for $200,000 to $300,000 beginning this year but acknowledged it occupies a legal "grey area."

"The whole world never had something like this before," he said.

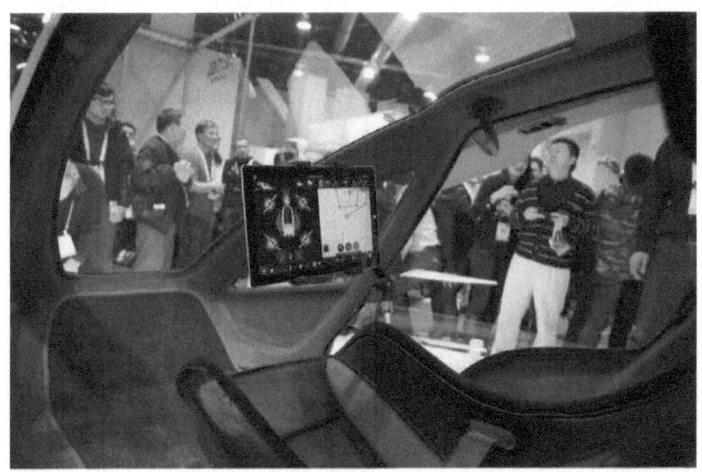

People crowd around the EHang 184 autonomous aerial vehicle at the EHang booth at CES International, Wednesday, Jan. 6, 2016, in Las Vegas. The drone is large enough to fit a human passenger (AP Photo/John Locher).

"A passenger would have no controls as a backup," he said. "In the event of a problem, the company plans a remote control center that would take over the vehicle and ensure it lands safely," he said.

Chief Marketing Officer Derrick Xiong said the vehicle has been flown more than one hundred times at low altitudes in a forested area in Guangzhou, including several times with a person inside.

"One thing that makes quad-copters safer than helicopters are its numerous propellers," Xiong said. Even if three of the four arms have their six propellers disabled, the final arm's working propellers can ensure a rough landing by spiraling toward the ground, he said.

The company, which also makes smaller drones, said in August it had raised $42 million in capital from various investors including GP Capital, GGV Capital, ZhenFund and others, following $10 million in capital raised the previous year.

CHAPTER 7

Philosophies and Strategies

Financial security isn't just about numbers; it's about a mindset and a set of guiding principles. In this chapter, I'll share some core philosophies and strategies that have helped me on the road to success.

1. **Find Joy, Not Just Security:** Happiness isn't a byproduct of wealth; it's a journey in itself. While financial security brings peace of mind, focus on finding joy in your everyday life. This could involve spending time with loved ones, pursuing hobbies, or simply taking time to appreciate the small things. When you find activities that spark joy, you'll be more motivated to achieve your

financial goals because you'll have a clear vision of the life you want to build.

2. **Offer a Helping Hand:** When you reach a place of stability, extend a helping hand to others. Whether it's volunteering your time, offering guidance, or simply sharing your knowledge, giving back fosters a sense of community and strengthens the world around you. Helping others can also be incredibly rewarding, bringing a sense of purpose and fulfillment that money alone cannot buy.

3. **Avoid Greed, Embrace Sustainability:** Aim for financial security, not excessive wealth. Building a sustainable income and managing it responsibly will bring long-term benefits. Focus on building wealth gradually through consistent savings, smart investments, and responsible spending habits. Avoid get-rich-quick schemes and risky financial decisions that could jeopardize your progress.

   Legitimate Income Sources: Building wealth ethically is crucial. Explore legitimate income sources that align with your skills and interests. Research different career paths, consider freelancing opportunities, or explore ways to turn your hobbies into income streams. There are endless possibilities available; the key is to find something that is both fulfilling and financially sustainable.

4. **Ownership and Control:** Owning property, whether your home or investments, can provide a sense of security and control over your financial future. Homeownership can offer stability and potential for wealth creation

through appreciation. Investing in a diversified portfolio can generate passive income and help you reach your long-term financial goals. Remember, however, that ownership also comes with responsibilities, so ensure you do your research and understand the risks involved before making any investment decisions.

Your aim and survival are not as a soldier but to execute flawlessly as warriors. Empowering alternatives with various resources toward fractures of inflammation. Wholeheartedly, I agree that we need our own independence. However, everyone viewing this book reminds me you are AGT, which means American Got Talent. Despite arguments, each one of us needs one another. No island was built by one person alone. We do not work for companies; however, we work with people.

Ordinarily, some of us do not like constructive criticism. Generally, I have open arms to accept, extract, and apply methods of workmanship. In other words, tackle the objective that is presented to you, take steps and measurements to comply, and fly like an eagle holding your head up high. Every hot dish eventually cools down and realize that learning is part of the process of life. A practice to succeed is giving utmost respect, harmony, and kindness to people whether it's people you dislike or those who dislike. Treat negativity by placing it in the rearview mirror. My concept is I might lose the battle but not the war. God gives you good, better, and best. When life rips what you have out of your hands, you get better than the best.

For each battle that arises, take the initiative to analyze them and do not fight everyone. Leave some as lessons to strengthen your weak points. Your destiny outweighs your history. Blessings outweigh the negativity. Don't limit yourself to limit possibilities because you know everything allows the negativity to be what it is so you can move forward. As you walk up the stairs, you will see handrails to guide your steps.

Do something different and alluring when we encounter angry folks. Collectively, there are small fractions of resilience, which may reflect on others at some time. Expedite abundant skills by utilizing your mindset and motivating yourself. Team up with others you admire by channeling various extraordinary experiences into business ventures. Part of your success is working through battles and struggles. In that case, make sure you don't settle for anything less than a wonderful day. Elevate new horizons spreading out so far, building new beginnings and chapters. Ponder the ways to build and progressively promote concrete foundations of legacies. I am a spoken voice for the voiceless. Battles and strategies through struggles pause for the moment. Sit back and ponder; you may be the "exclusive leader" selected to aim toward the radar, head to spear obstacles, and face them. Endure, I highly recommend everyone channel and utilize your energy. Take note of productive works, for some must emphasize a transparency point and use variables.

Phantom Debt

(Growing strong in the United States. The fashion to buy now and pay later.)

https://youtu.be/bdpO_zWEYxU?si=xGlfiIlmzLk52n5Y

Interesting Engineering on UVeye – The MRI for Cars
https://youtu.be/zUwKdtXqTp4?si=53oiy2wCIswBFgs-

How to Beat Fear and Anxiety
https://youtu.be/bb9g9mtDHZo?si=6N-JkCF_YL8e7i_P

Be Patient to Start Small While Thinking Big - Vusi Thembekwayo
https://youtu.be/gNfCeDjE9xI?si=QtNud2TDfhBUBT6v

Phantom Debt Growing Strong in the United States
(The fashion to buy now and pay later)
https://youtu.be/bdpO_zWEYxU?si=xGlfiIlmzLk52n5Y

Powerful Manifesting Techniques Real Life Examples
https://youtu.be/EJZcly3wvTk

Giving Patients a Second Chance with Prosthetics | New Series: Body Parts
https://youtu.be/c7YSfCfPEp8?si=Xh212bwNTOTLRSEV

Alison Bess – Clinical Anaplastologist
https://youtu.be/VhzY3-AKaVE

Victoria Tries on Her New Hands | Body Parts
https://youtu.be/tPWUy7DPz4k?si=HdDxy1dGZi5nDy-x

Article References

Janie Deegan, She Was Drug Addicted, and Now She Owns Three Bakeries in New York
(Her statement I liked was "Don't quit before the miracle.")
https://youtu.be/8BfuNrhrv_I?si=-0hayi8iJTNAYaAS

Dr. Wayne Dyer - Relax and You Will Manifest Anything You Desire
https://youtu.be/R6PGrTFrFzQ?si=Q5HMbn3peLj9vfcu

Ushering in matters of a wide range for let us go and flow with a tremendous main focus. Generally, some of us are uncertain the purpose we revolve here on earth. Our lives interact various channels of finance. Debts we occur through times of harsh hardships.

Nevertheless, we all should represent an overflow building a substantial foundation. Utilizing tools to build a Command Of Excellence. An interaction proactively to open shut doors methods of utilizing keys of knowledge on a journey in life as my theory known as "COD" (Cancelation Of Debt).

Typically, I do not feel a revolution to break through bound chains by success while you suffer.

Logically a spectacular way to navigate through particular vital resources that you view completely do your research taking ample time and patience.

Michael Bloomberg is the 15th richest person in the world and is worth an estimated $106.2 billion. Part of a blessing is to give to others Bloomberg's Footprints which I wish to follow.

Source: Forbes

<u>Mike Bloomberg Donates $1 Billion To Cover Tuition For Most Johns Hopkins Medical Students</u>

Man with Golden Voice, Ted Williams, One Year after Shooting to Fame

By Jordan Chittley | <u>Daily Buzz</u> – Thu, 12 Jan, 2012

Just over a year ago (1.6.11) when the world first saw Ted Williams, he was homeless and standing at the side of a road holding a sign that said he had a great voice.

Now the man with the golden voice has a much different look. He has a clean haircut, glasses, is no longer wearing a camouflage jacket and is living under a roof.

Williams shot to fame after the Columbus Dispatch newspaper posted a video shot by Doral Chenoweth. Williams was standing at the side of a road with a sign that read, "I have a God given gift of voice." Curious, Chenoweth asked Williams to say something and the video took off.

Chenoweth caught up with Williams at the end of last month and said he has completed a three-month drug rehabilitation program, is off the streets and is working. He is living just outside Columbus, Ohio in Dublin and is doing voice-overs for a Boston-based cable network.

The TV show Entertainment Tonight also met up with Williams as he celebrated a year after his video went viral.

"A year ago today I was living in tents under bridges, smoking crack, doing all the wild things," he said in the video. Now he has a fireplace, a flat-screen TV and a walk-in closet that doubles as a recording studio.

"What a difference a year makes," he said as he admits to not being able to dream of living in a spacious home more than a year ago. "It's a halleluiah moment every day I wake up."

But it hasn't been an easy year for Williams as he shot to fame. Shortly after the video went viral, the Ohio paper that posted the video was inundated with calls and emails offering Williams opportunities. The Cleveland Cavaliers offered him a full-time job doing voice over work and offered to pay the mortgage on a home. He also made the rounds on national morning shows including one where he reunited with his mother.

However, the quick fame appeared to be too much for Williams to handle.

Less than a week after the video went viral, he was detained by police in Hollywood after being involved in a verbal altercation with his daughter in a hotel room. They were staying at the hotel prior to an appearance on the Dr. Phil show. Williams reunited with his ex-wife and five of his nine children on the show.

The day after the Dr. Phil show announced Williams was heading to rehab. "(Williams) agreed to go to a private facility following a lengthy one-on-one conversation with Dr. Phil," read a statement issued by the show.

"I've told him it's not going to be easy and it's going to take a lot of hard work," said Dr. Phil in the statement in an Access Hollywood article. "It might be a long journey for him, but this is a big step in the right direction."

In the twenty years prior to becoming an overnight Internet sensation, **Williams had been charged with robbery, escape, forgery and drug possession.**

Now, both Chenoweth and ET report Williams is sober and doing much better.

His book titled A Golden Voice: How faith, hard work and humility brought me from the streets to salvation is set to be released in May.

Empowering Everyone's Storms Of Inflation In Life: Make In Shrinkation

I have never been more impressed and inspired by anyone in my life as I have been from you. I rate the opportunity to meet and hear you speak as one of the top 10 moments of my life so far. — Venki Prathivadi, Head of Australia & New Zealand for Mahindra Satyam

Who is Jessica Cox?

Jessica is recognized internationally as an inspirational keynote speaker. Born without arms, Jessica now flies airplanes, drives cars and otherwise lives a normal life using her feet as others use their hands. She holds the title of the first person without arms in the American Taekwondo Association to get a black belt and the Guinness World Record for being the first armless person in aviation history to earn a pilot's certificate. Convinced that the way we think has a greater impact on our lives than our physical constraints, she chose to pursue a degree in psychology at the University of Arizona. Since then she has traveled to 17 countries sharing her inspirational message.

If Jessica can fly a plane with only her feet, what can you do?

Armless Girl Jessica Cox Gains Pilot's License

Summary:

Email forward tells the inspirational story of Jessica Cox, a girl who was able to gain her pilot's license, among other remarkable achievements, in spite of being born without arms (Full commentary below).

CHAPTER 8

Employment Opportunities

The foundation of financial security often lies in a fulfilling career. This chapter equips you with the tools to navigate the vast landscape of employment opportunities and identify the path that aligns with your skills, interests, and financial goals.

Before diving into specific jobs, embark on a journey of self-discovery. Ask yourself:

- What are my strengths and passions?
- Or if you are feeling more serious, reflect back to Chapter 2 and ask yourself what is my purpose on this earth?

- Do you enjoy working with your hands, solving problems, or interacting with people? Identifying your natural talents will help you excel in your chosen career.
- What work environment best suits me? Do you thrive in fast-paced, collaborative settings or prefer independent work with a focus on detail? Understanding your work style preferences will guide you toward a comfortable and productive career path.
- What is my desired salary and lifestyle? Certain careers offer higher earning potential while others provide more flexibility or work-life balance. Determining your financial goals and desired lifestyle will help you prioritize when exploring job options.

Exploring Career Paths

With a clearer picture of your aspirations, delve into different career paths. Here, we'll explore a few broad categories, but remember, this is not an exhaustive list, just a suggestion that can spark a lightbulb in your mind guiding you to a potential industry:

So let's start with industries that are thriving and won't grow obsolete in the near future because who hates an everlasting career that is not under threat by AI or robots?

Healthcare: This ever-growing sector offers diverse roles, from doctors and nurses to technicians and therapists. Consider specializations like geriatrics, mental health, or medical technology.

Science and Technology: If you have an analytical mind and a passion for innovation, explore careers in engineering, software development, data science, or cybersecurity, these fields are constantly evolving, offering exciting opportunities to be at the forefront of progress.

Business and Finance: This sector caters to individuals with strong organizational and analytical skills. Explore possibilities in accounting, finance, marketing, human resources, or project management.

Emerging Frontiers

Renewable Energy: As the world prioritizes sustainability, careers in solar energy, wind power, and other green technologies are in high demand.

Cybersecurity: The need for cybersecurity experts to protect data and systems in our increasingly digital world is paramount.

Artificial Intelligence and Robotics: This rapidly developing field offers opportunities for researchers, engineers, and software developers shaping the future of AI and robotics.

Beyond Traditional Jobs

However, the modern world is not boring and stagnant; it offers a multitude of nontraditional career paths:

The Gig Economy or basically where you can hustle or earn extra cash: Platforms like Uber, Lyft, and Fiverr connect individuals with freelance work opportunities, allowing for flexibility and autonomy. Air BnB, but beforehand, view your local state's laws and regulations.

Content Creation: Are you a skilled writer, photographer, or videographer? Explore content creation through social media platforms, blogs, or online marketplaces.

Or if you are a person who has an idea, try to make your own business. Delve into entrepreneurship. Do you have a unique idea and the drive to build it? Entrepreneurship can be a rewarding path, but it requires dedication, resilience, and a solid business plan. But whatever you do . . .

- **Research Thoroughly**—Explore informational interviews with professionals, attend career fairs, and utilize online resources.
- **Network Effectively**—Build connections with people in your desired field. LinkedIn can be a valuable tool.
- **Invest in Your Development**—Consider taking additional courses or pursuing certifications to enhance your skills and marketability.

I don't mean to say you'll know what to do because, trust me, with so many new careers coming up, we are all overwhelmed and finding the right career path is a process—don't be afraid to explore different options. By aligning your skills, passions, and values with the vast array of opportunities available, you can build a fulfilling and financially rewarding career.

New York Safety Educator – Driving Instructor Sponsorship Program

As a certified New York and New Jersey Driving Defense Instructor. The New York Safety Educator Sponsorship, which the public can benefit by savings. Plus, those who participate in this assist me build in the future a New York driving school base, from which everyone benefits.

Actually, we sponsor driver instructors on job training with pay, assistance, and support from the public contributions of $27.00 (Bill Payment / Checks/ Money Orders payable made to New York Safety Educator mailing address James A. Farly Building Station PO Box 8162 New York, NY 10116-8162) or another method of payment Zelle Payment (email address: newyorksafetyeducator@gmail.com). All donations are tax-deductible.

Our objective is to establish a driving school in New York. Once approved, we are offering exclusive employment as follows:

- Medical Benefits
- Hire Veterans
- Approved Waiver Exemption by the State of New York Applicants with Felony
- Promote Part-Time Driver Instructors
- Employment for Managers
- Employment for Administrators
- Prospective Churches' Members
- Hire Part-Time Disabled Workers
- Hire Part-Time Seniors

New York Safety Educator is a Driving Defense Course that provides an automobile and motorcycle reduction of 10 percent discount insurance. Basically, New York drivers and New Jersey drivers both are entitled to be issued benefits for up to three years.

Ultimately, we are working to establish a New York driving school. Drivers who possess a valid New York driver's license with a minimum of two years' experience, no moving violations, no points, high school diploma, or GED; and these qualifications are applicable to be established as a driving instructor.

New York State Department of Motor Vehicles
Approved Defensive Driving on Line Course *
10% Reduction Insurance
3 Years
$29.95

Automobile or Motorcycle
Liability and Collision Insurance
Driving Record Reduction
(Eligibility up to 4 Points)

New York State Driver
New York Safety Educator—Driving Instructor Sponsorship Program

Actually, we sponsor Driver Instructors on job training with pay, assistance, and support from the public *contributions of $27.00* (Bill Payment / Checks/ Money Orders payable made to *New York Safety Educator mailing address James A. Farley Building Station P.O. Box 8162 New York, NY 10116-8162*) or another method of payment Zelle Payment (email address *newyorksafetyeducator@gmail.com*). All donations are tax-deductible.

Our objective is to establish a driving school in New York once approved we are offering exclusive employment as follows:

. New Yorkers Who Qualifies For Medical Benefits
. Hire Veterans
. Approved Waiver Exemption By The State of New York Applicants With Felony
. Promote Part-Time Driver Instructors
· Employment For Managers
. Employment For Administrators
· Prospective Churches' Members
· Hire Part-Time Disable Workers
· Hire Part-Time Seniors

New York Safety Educator is a Driving Defense Course which provides an automobile and motorcycle reduction of 10% discount insurance. Basically, New York Drivers and New Jersey Drivers both are entitled to be issued benefits up to 3 years.

Ultimately, we are working to establish a New York Driving School. Drivers who possess a valid New York Driver's license with a minimum of 2 years' experience; no moving violations; no points; high school diploma; GED; and these qualifications are applicable to be established as a Driving Instructor.

New York State Department Of Motor Vehicles
Approved Defensive Driving On Line Course *
10% Reduction Insurance
3 Years
$29.95
Automobile Or Motorcycle
Liability & Collision Insurance
Driving Record Reduction
(*Eligibility Up To 4 Points*)

New York State Driver
Promotion Code: 7777
- Register On Website –
http://empiresafetycouncil.com

Greetings!

Empire Safety Council Inc. offers the online course in the amount of $44.95; however, there is a $15.00 deduction once you register and input *promotion code 7777* your discount would be

Empowering Everyone's Storms Of Inflation In Life: Make In Shrinkation

$29.95. Ultimately, anyone who is a New Jersey driver can use same website and scroll down the next box under New York.

After completion of the course kindly leave an email at NewYorkSafeyEducator@gmail.com keep in mind that Empire Safety Council's DDC is recognized and approved by all New York and New Jersey insurance carriers *any problems contact Empire Safety Council at (631) 360-2160.*

New York Drivers Registration Reference

    A. Scroll down to box New York Defense Driving Online Course

    B. Click to Register

    C. Click pay after your register

    D. View Terms and Conditions / Privacy Policy

    E. Scroll at the bottom of box and type *I agree*

    F. Click Go to Registration

    G. Sign up

New Jersey Drivers Registration Reference

    A. Scroll down to box New Jersey Defensive Driving Online Course

    B. Click to Register

    C. Click pay after your register

    D. View Terms and Conditions / Privacy Policy

    E. Scroll at the bottom of box and type *I agree*

    F. Click Go to Registration

    G. Sign up

Glenn Colson

New York Safety Educator Distributions to Participate

Incentive Sponsorship Program

Once We Reach Our Goal

1,000,000 Participates

First 500 New Yorkers

Will Receive $100.00

First 500 New Jersey

Will Receive $100.00

Upon Completion of Course

Empowering Everyone's Storms Of Inflation In Life: Make In Shrinkation

Why should I take your driving defense course?

Let's discuss the benefits!

New York **Safety Educator**

Empowering Everyone's Storms Of Inflation In Life: Make In Shrinkation

Glenn Colson

Empowering Everyone's Storms Of Inflation In Life: Make In Shrinkation

Glenn Colson

Empowering Everyone's Storms Of Inflation In Life: Make In Shrinkation

Glenn Colson

Empowering Everyone's Storms Of Inflation In Life: Make In Shrinkation

Glenn Colson

Empowering Everyone's Storms Of Inflation In Life: Make In Shrinkation

Glenn Colson

Empowering Everyone's Storms Of Inflation In Life: Make In Shrinkation

Glenn Colson

Empowering Everyone's Storms Of Inflation In Life: Make In Shrinkation

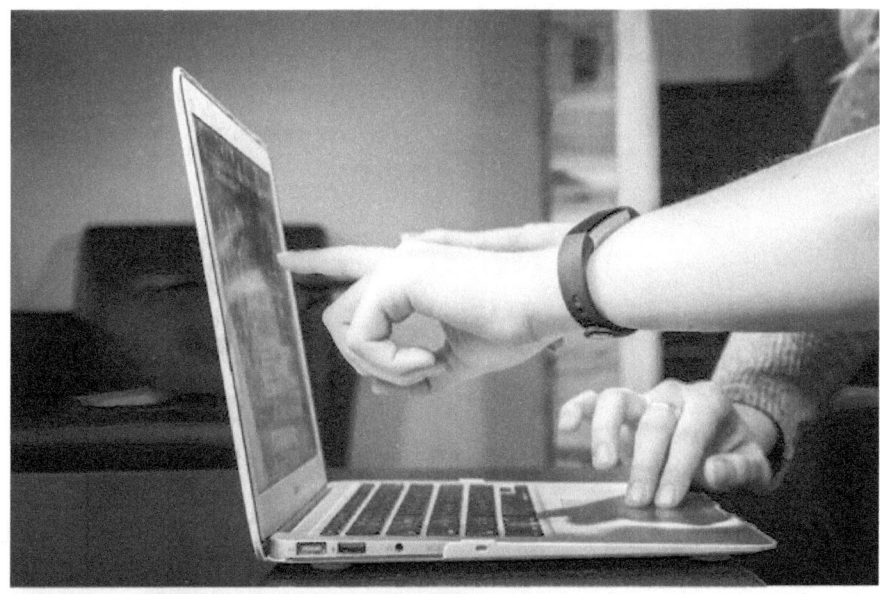

Glenn Colson

Empowering Everyone's Storms Of Inflation In Life: Make In Shrinkation

Glenn Colson

Empowering Everyone's Storms Of Inflation In Life: Make In Shrinkation

Glenn Colson

Empowering Everyone's Storms Of Inflation In Life: Make In Shrinkation

Glenn Colson

Empowering Everyone's Storms Of Inflation In Life: Make In Shrinkation

Glenn Colson

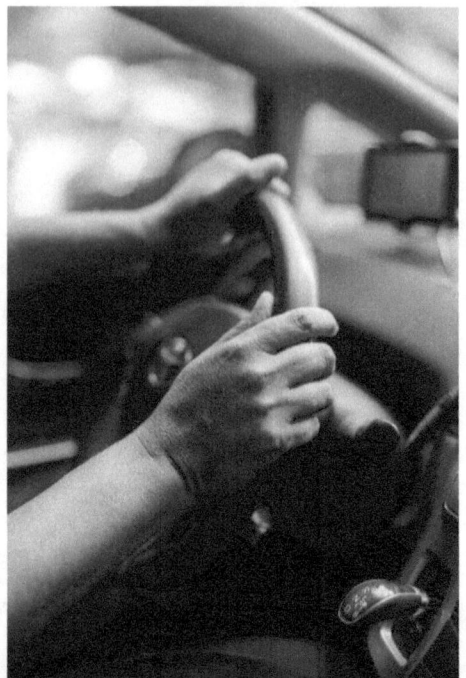

Empowering Everyone's Storms Of Inflation In Life: Make In Shrinkation

CHAPTER 9

Conclusion

We've come a long way together, exploring the path toward achieving financial security. Throughout this book, we've explored budgeting strategies, debt management techniques, and the importance of building wealth. As we come to the end of this journey, I want to leave you with a powerful message: achieving financial well-being is within your grasp.

By gaining knowledge and tools throughout this book, you can make informed financial decisions. Remember, financial literacy is a lifelong journey. Continue to learn and adapt as your circumstances evolve.

Significant change often begins with small, consistent actions. Stick to your budget, automate your savings, and prioritize debt repayment. Over time, these seemingly small steps will lead to financial stability.

The road to financial security isn't always smooth. Unexpected expenses, setbacks, and periods of temptation may arise. However, if you remember your goals, stay focused, and don't be afraid to seek help when needed, you will overcome any challenges.

Why You Need This Book (Especially Now) in the Face of Persistent Inflation

The world is facing a new reality: inflation isn't a temporary blip. It's here to stay, at least for the foreseeable future. This means the cost of everything from groceries to gas to rent is steadily rising, squeezing household budgets and threatening financial security.

That's Where This Book Comes In. It's not just a guide to financial well-being; it's a lifeline in these times of rising prices. Here's why this book is crucial for navigating every aspect of your life (all ambits) in the face of inflation:

- **The Budget Blueprint**: Regularly revisit your budget to ensure it reflects your current income and expenses. Adjust as needed to maintain financial equilibrium.
- **The Debt-Conquest Plan:** Stay committed to your debt repayment strategy. Celebrate milestones and reward yourself for achieving financial goals, but don't deviate from your plan.
- **The Wealth-Building Compass**: Investing for the future is crucial. Research different investment options,

diversify your portfolio, and leverage the power of compound interest to grow your wealth over time.
- **Inflation Impacts Every Area of Life:** From your daily commute to your monthly groceries, it affects your decisions and purchasing power. Financial literacy is a key weapon in breaking the cycle of poverty. By sharing the knowledge and strategies outlined in this book, we can empower future generations to build a secure financial future.

Financial stability and independence are achievable goals. Embrace the power within you, utilize the tools at your disposal, and never stop believing in your ability to achieve financial freedom.

Dial up your approach toward negativity, which you should roll around and chase out the window and replace it with good matters. A great perspective is embracing gratitude of thanks and positive thoughts, evicting a battle of defeated forces of destruction, and using the best defense with offense. Thoughts should empower you by erasing doubt.

I just want to leave you with one last thought, the journey continues beyond the last page of this book. Keep learning, keep growing, and embrace the bright financial future that awaits you.

Index

A

Abbott, Gregory Wayne 38
Airlines Discounts 21
Article References 108
Aviation Programs 26

B

Boone, David 97-8
Brown, Wanda 48, 52-3
Buffet, Warren 93-6
Bullying 7, 45
Bush, Grace 86-9

C

Carjacking vii, 8
Carter, Henrietta 48
Colson, Annie 52
Colson, Glenn vii, 2, 4, 6, 8, 10, 14, 16, 18, 20, 22, 24, 26, 28, 30
Colson, Roz 41
Colson, Yolanda 41
Community Organizations 39
Company Policies 45
Coopetition 4
Cox, Jessica 62-6, 68-73, 113-14
Criticism 37

D

Darling, Sarah 82
Depression, how to combat 9-10
Destruction 41, 152
Diana 38
Discrimination 7, 42-4
Driving School 120-1

E

Ehang 184 99-102
Employment Opportunities 115, 117-19

F

Fields-Witherspoon Mitchell, Michele 48-9
Financial planning 12-14
Financial security 103-7, 115
Five Ps xxiv, 48
FlexJobs 27-8
Florida Whiz Kid 86-7

G

Gatekeepers 34-5
Grande, Richard 51

H

Harassment 44
Harris, Billy Ray 81-2
Heyward, Diana 40
Huerta, Michael 100

I

Inflation 1-4, 6-9, 11-13, 15, 17, 19, 21, 23, 25, 27, 29, 31, 33, 35, 151
International Labor Organization (ILO) 44-6
Investments 13-15, 104, 151

J

Jamaican John 53-4
James, Glen 79-81
Job Search Resources 29

K

Kaiser Permanente School of Medicine 17
King, Martin Luther, Jr. 7
Krejci, Bill 82

L

Laws, national 45
Leach, Ollie B. 52
Legal Protection, Challenges and Considerations 47
Legal Protections 42

M

Mandela, Nelson 7
Manufacturing Principles 3
Marriage, questions to ask before 43

McCardel, Chloe 77
Modeste, Lovejoy 49
Mutual Omaha Company 47

N

National Alliance on Mental Illness (NAMI) 11
Negativity 36
New York City Police Department 23, 53
New York Safety Educator 119-22
Nyad, Diana 57-8, 75-7

P

Parks, Rosa 7
Prenuptial Agreements 43-4
Property, Owning 104
Public Service References 20, 22-3

R

Ramirez Romero, Ruth Marisol 49-50
Rodriguez, Eddie 36, 49
Ruiz, Jessica 89-91

S

Self-Sufficiency Standard Institute (SSTI) 34
Self-Wounds 50
Senior Citizen Rent Increase Exemption (SCRIE) 23
Sexual Harassment 45
Shang Hsiao 101
Small Business Services 24
Smith, Margaret 73-4, 84-5
Sponsorship Program 119
Struggles, Financial 10-11

Substance Abuse and Mental Health Services (SAMHSA) 11

T

Traweek, Parrish 66-7
Turtle 37

U

UR Nursing Scholars Program 19-21

V

Volunteering 50-1

W

Wealth-Building 104, 150
Williams, Ted 58-61, 110-12
Winfred 38

Y

Yarborough, Olene 48

www.ingramcontent.com/pod-product-compliance
Lightning Source LLC
Chambersburg PA
CBHW020655220526
45464CB00001B/438